The Armageddon Network

MICHAEL P. SABA

Edited by Evan Hendricks

Amana Books
Vermont 1984

Copyright© 1984 by Michael P. Saba
All rights reserved. No part of this book may be reproduced or utilized in
any form or by any means without permission in writing from the author.
Inquiries may be addressed to Michael Saba c/o Amana Books, 58 Elliot
Street, Brattleboro, Vermont 05301.

Library of Congress catalog card number: 84-072241
ISBN: 0-915597-07-1
First Edition

Cover Design by Rakan Jawdat

For my father, Naif Saba, who knew
the truth before others,
And for my children, Miriamah and Jesse,
who will benefit from the truth being told.

FOREWORD

What you are about to read is first a spy story. It involves, in the classic pattern, the apparent misappropriation of highly classified documents belonging to the U.S. Department of Defense and unauthorized dissemination of these materials to a foreign government.

Moreover, this was not a minor security compromise. The Defense Intelligence Agency has officially determined, as the following pages will reveal, that the incident described has involved information the disclosure of which could adversely affect the essential national security interests of the United States, including U.S. relations with several Middle Eastern nations, U.S. intelligence collection activities, future U.S. arms sales negotiations and authorized U.S. intelligence exchanges with foreign governments.

That those involved in this affair are still "at large," and in fact currently hold senior positions in the Pentagon, is what distinguishes *The Armageddon Network* from the average non-fiction account of an espionage investigation. For this is an unfinished story of a possible coverup and effort to abort the normal investigatory and prosecutorial processes that swung into motion after the incident was brought to the attention of the U.S. Department of Justice [DOJ].

Whether the evidence in this case warranted prosecution cannot be finally determined until more facts are revealed by the Criminal Investigation Division at the Department of Justice. What is certain, however, is that incredible pressure was brought to bear upon the Federal Bureau of Investigation and other sections at the DOJ to terminate the investigation, and upon news media who were covering the case to prevent publication of the details of the affair. Ultimately, the pressure prevailed, and it is largely for this reason that the story is only now being told, seven years after the event itself.

By this time wary readers will have guessed, if they did not already know, that the "foreign government" involved here is the State of Israel, a presumed and frequent ally of the United States, particularly as regards Soviet penetration of the Middle East. Thus we have another unusual dimension in the story, for the individuals involved in this apparent "unauthorized disclosure" of classified information probably genuinely felt they were serving not only the national security interests of Israel, but those of the United States as well. The Defense Intelligence Agency did not agree.

Edward Crankshaw has written in his foreword to *The Penkovskiy Papers* that:

> . . . . a man who will take it upon himself to betray his
> government because he is uniquely convinced that he
> is right and they are wrong is by definition unbalanced,
> although he may also be a martyr.

This, it seems to me, is an essential point about the U.S. Government officials who are the objects of the investigation described in this book. It matters little whether they were/are well motivated. Their zeal, their lack of balance in their desire to assist Israel, seems to have warped their judgment where U.S. interests are concerned.

I can personally attest, on the basis of recent personal interviews, that senior Middle East leaders are fully aware of both the specific incidents described herein, and the pervasive pattern of U.S. security indiscretions where Israel is concerned. This knowledge, as much as the public security agreements between America and Israel in the past 2-3 years, has changed the way these leaders approach their own security plans vis-a-vis the United States, Western Europe and the Eastern Bloc countries.

Even Egypt, to which the U.S. post-Camp David has provided over a billion dollars in military aid annually, has recently begun to operate on the premise that American advice and advisors constitute an Israeli Trojan horse in their midst. A careful reading of *The Armageddon Network* will show the accuracy and wisdom of this assumption.

This book also convincingly explains how American commercial as well as security relationships are adversely affected by the activities of Israel's special interest leaders in Washington, both inside and outside the Government, and how Soviet interests are correspondingly advanced. In a sense the Soviets, who for religious and historical reasons have very little affinity with the countries of the Middle East, are now being given a second lease on life in the region. Herein rests the penultimate irony of the efforts of Israel's friends, most of whom also profess a virulent forum of anti-communism.

The ultimate irony, of course, is the effect which Israel's American friends are having upon the health and prosperity of the State of Israel itself.

Stephen Green
author of *Taking Sides :
America's Secret Relations with
a Militant Israel*
August 7, 1984

Contents

Acknowledgements

It would take another book to thank everyone who helped to tell this story. In the six years I have been following this case, numerous individuals have been of great assistance and I thank them all. Special thanks go to Irene Hansen, Piney Kesting, Paula Stinson, and Daud Malik Watts.

INTRODUCTION

This book is the result of a personal odyssey which began on the fateful day of March 9, 1978, and continues into the present. The manner in which I came to know of Stephen D. Bryen can be viewed as an act of destiny, good luck or misfortune — depending upon your point of view. No matter what you call it, the chance encounter in which I overheard Bryen speaking candidly with Israeli defense officials has had dramatic consequences for me. For one, it has prompted me to examine the rise to power of what I consider to be a dangerous network of power-hungry individuals. It has also caused me to change my view of the American Government and its conduct of international affairs.

The purpose of this book is not to "convict" anyone or to serve as a substitute trial. These are the tasks of the American system of justice — of law enforcers, prosecutors and courts. However, this book does examine how our system of justice functioned in Stephen Bryen's case, and it probes the implications of that case. *The Armageddon Network* also illustrates how the special treatment of Bryen reflects the American Government's special treatment of Israel and examines the "policy of exceptionalism." Both Bryen and Israel are working to achieve U.S. policies that benefit Israel, but which are more and more damaging to America both at home and abroad.

This book focuses on Deputy Assistant Secretary of Defense Stephen Bryen, Assistant Secretary of Defense Richard Perle, and their closest associates, and serves as a case study of the problems inherent in the current U.S. policy of unquestioning support of Israel.

But what the reader must remember is that Bryen and Perle are part of a larger network of influential officials who act as if "What is good for Israel is good for the United States." The network is not necessarily directed from a central point. It is more likely that the members merely share the same commitment to seeing Israel put first — regardless of the costs to the United States and the world. The network includes high-level officials throughout all agencies of government, Congressional aides, and journalists and other media specialists who cut or avoid stories which present Israel in a negative light and promote attempts to smear Israel's "enemies."

The ultimate question centers on where the network promoting the "Israel-first" policy is taking America. Perle and Bryen are leading hawks in a very hawkish Administration. They push more guns, bombs, and missiles as the mainstay of their hardline policies. The problem is that this promises to exacerbate tensions in an already unstable Middle East. The region seems more and more like a time bomb waiting to explode. Promoting U.S. military "strategic cooperation" with Israel, rather than negotiation, reminds me of Carl Sagan's story about walking into a room full of gasoline and lighting a match.

As a result of geography, energy needs, religion and history, the Middle East will never be an isolated region. Rather, it will always play an important role in determining the fate of the entire world. It is the home of the biblical site of Armageddon, which carries horrific connotations of the end of the world. From what I have seen in the last six years, Richard Perle and Stephen Bryen and the network of people who share their cause continue to consistently promote policies that will resurrect Armageddon as the final battlefield for the Middle East — and the world.

As I mentioned, my examination of Bryen and Perle is merely a case study of a much larger problem. It represents only a sliver off the tip of the iceberg. It is a story that raises more questions than it answers. Perhaps its true value is that it attempts to raise the right questions.

CHAPTER 1

CHANCE ENCOUNTER AT THE MADISON HOTEL

March 9, 1978, began as a routine day. I was President of a North Dakota company promoting international trade and had just returned to Washington, D.C. from an overseas trip. I had scheduled a 9:00 A.M. business meeting with a potential client at the Madison Hotel Coffee Shop, not far from Capitol Hill. I arrived thirty minutes early. The coffee shop hostess seated me at a corner table and I started reading the newspaper to pass the time.

I looked up from the newspaper and noticed three men sitting at the adjacent table about ten feet away. The moustached man in the pinstripe suit facing me looked vaguely familiar. But I had worked in Washington as Executive Director of the National Association of Arab Americans for the previous two years, and the city was full of familiar faces.

A few minutes later, however, another man entered and the trio at the table rose to their feet. The man who seemed familiar was introduced as "Stephen Bryen of the Senate Foreign Relations Committee." Two of the men began speaking in Hebrew. The remaining introductions indicated that the other men were officials of the Israeli Government. With the pleasantries aside, they sat down and began what was obviously a very serious business discussion.

I did not pay much attention to the group at first, but

proximity and Stephen Bryen's tone of voice made it impossible not to overhear their conversation. As the dialogue progressed, it became obvious that they were discussing actual strategies to influence U.S. policy in favor of Israel. I thought it odd that a Senate Foreign Relations Committee staffer would have this sort of conversation with officials of a foreign government, and so I began to discreetly take notes of what they were saying. Little did I know at the time that what I was about to hear — and the events which followed — would lead me down a path of inquiry which would reveal to me the activities of a small group of influential U.S. policy-makers who used their positions to shape American policy — regardless of the economic and strategic costs — so as to favor the military interests of the Israeli Government. Ultimately, it would reveal to me the full extent of America's dangerous and tragic policies toward Israel and the threat those policies pose to world peace.

But such philosophical thoughts were not on my mind as this coffee shop meeting took place before me. I concentrated on accurately writing down everything that was being said. Bryen was doing most of the talking.

In 1978, conflict in the Middle East was as intense as ever. Tension was high on the Israeli-occupied West Bank. Jordan recently had deployed I-Hawk missiles. Saudi Arabia was building additional air force bases. The Carter Administration was considering the sale of F-15 fighter jets to Egypt and the Saudis. Although the Camp David accords were still seven months away, I later learned that it was on this day that the Israelis first revealed to Bryen the key demands which they would later present to American negotiators.

As Bryen lectured the Israelis, what struck me immediately was the way in which he used the pronoun "we" to embrace his own position and that of the Israelis, and the pronoun "they" to describe the United States, the Carter Administration and Congressional members who questioned a policy of unconditional support of Israel.[1]* Whose side was he on, anyway?

He first instructed the Israelis, who were high-level defense officials, that they were losing a lot of credibility with Congress and the Administration because Prime Minister Menachem Begin insisted on invoking religious and historical grounds for seizing the West Bank. Despite arguments from the Israelis, Bryen insisted, "We must re-establish credibility. The West Bank can be gained on security grounds. To get Jackson [Senator Henry Jackson of Washington] and the others back, we must push the security issue."[2]

He said they should tell their boss, Ezer Weizman, the Israeli Defense Minister who at the same time was meeting across the street with editors of the *Washington Post*,[3] to publicly advocate security reasons. "This is the only argument that would help us to keep the West Bank, and we must push it, and we must get people like Weizman to make a statement at this point," Bryen said.[4]

When one man mentioned that President Carter had criticized Israel for its West Bank policies, Bryen told him, "Never let the President of the United States get away with these kinds of statements." He added, "This Administration is so pig-headed that we have to deal differently."[5]

Another Israeli joined the group. They all shook hands and spoke in Hebrew. It was not clear whether Bryen was following their conversation.

The focus shifted to the Carter Administration's plan to sell jet fighters to Egypt, Saudi Arabia and Israel. Bryen took charge again and informed them of key Senators on the Senate Foreign Relations Committee. "They think they have

---

* See Appendix A for Affidavit of Michael P. Saba

[Frank] Church, and have neutralized [Henry] Jackson, but Henry wouldn't make a deal without talking to us about it," he said.[6]

The Israelis expressed concern about getting the arms they wanted from the United States. "We can make them bargain," Bryen replied.[7]

Then came Bryen's key statement. An Israeli asked Bryen whether certain information was available. He responded, "I have the Pentagon document on the bases, which you are welcome to see."[8]

It was a statement that would haunt him for several years to come. Little did I know at the time that the Pentagon document to which Bryen probably referred was top-secret material on the defense systems of Middle East countries, described by the U.S. Defense Intelligence Agency as extremely valuable information to the Israelis.

The conversation returned to the proposed sale of jet fighters to Egypt and the Saudis. Bryen advised them that the National Security Council was the pivotal player and said, "We need to get inside the bargain with Brzezinski.* The main thing to do is to make a deal in the National Security Council. We should play for the compromise." After discussing strategies to secure a compromise, Bryen declared, "Our best bet is Erich von Marbod.** He's the military sales guy on the deal ... He looks German but he's with us."[9] The Israelis, apparently not familiar with von Marbod, seemed glad to hear they had someone so dependable in the U.S. Defense Department.

Bryen advised them to be realistic about their chances. "We can't stop the Egyptian part, but perhaps we could halt the sale

---

*Zbigniew Brzezinski, National Security Advisor to President Jimmy Carter.

**Erich von Marbod was then the Deputy Director of the Defense Security Assistance Agency.

of aircraft to the Saudis," he said.

As for Israel's needs, the group discussed the technology Israel would need so it could manufacture its own jet fighters and avoid the high cost of buying them from the United States. "I hope you have good R & D and get ready to convert it into weapons," Bryen said, referring to "research and development."[10]

Bryen told them about a specific aircraft. "It's not a bad airplane. I've flown in it myself. Can you make it yourself?" he asked.[11]

"Yes, we don't have to buy it," replied an Israeli.

"Good, then we're all right there," Bryen concluded. "I've got to get back to the Hill."[12]

The group adjourned, exchanged goodbyes, and walked out of the coffee shop. I gathered my thoughts and realized that I needed to recall everything as precisely as possible. For the next hour I sat there, transcribing my notes. By this time I had forgotten completely that my original purpose for going to the coffee shop was a business meeting. As fate would have it, the appointment never showed up.

With my notes transcribed, I spent the rest of the day and night thinking about the incident. What was most disturbing to me was that Bryen seemed to be putting his loyalties to Israel ahead of his loyalties to the government of the taxpayers who paid his salary. At the time, it did not occur to me that Bryen may have actually violated the law. I knew the event was important, however, and felt that some authority should be notified of it.

But I was uncertain as to where to go. If I saw someone stealing I could report it to the police. But to which agency of the United States Government's machinery does one go with this kind of information? Finally, I decided to seek the advice of Jim Abourezk, the Democratic Senator from South Dakota. I knew that he could refer me to the proper authority.

Although the ties between the Abourezks and my family extended back to our parents, it was not until the 1970s when I moved to Washington and Jim was elected Senator that we actually met and became friends. Our friendship had strengthened over the years, and I trusted Jim to give me sound advice about what I should do with the information I had overheard.

When I called Abourezk the next morning, he agreed to see me and scheduled me for a lunch appointment. When I told him about what had transpired at the Madison Hotel, he was extremely concerned about the implications it could have for United States security and the U.S. position in the Middle East. He stressed that the affair could have very serious ramifications both in the U.S. and abroad, and advised me to report the incident to the Justice Department immediately.

Senator Abourezk agreed to facilitate a meeting for me with Benjamin Civiletti, then Assistant Attorney General for the Criminal Division. Civiletti scheduled an appointment for me for the same afternoon. The Attorney General would obviously be concerned about a possible breach of security.

I also decided to bring the story to the attention of the media. I concluded that the best prospects were the *Washington Post* and columnist Jack Anderson. I was sure that the *Post*, as the major paper in the nation's capital, would be highly interested in what I had to say about Bryen and his meeting. After all, it was the *Post* that just a few years earlier had uncovered the Watergate scandal, one of the greatest conspiracies of modern American political history. By 3:00 that afternoon, Larry Stern of the *Post* and Joe Speer from Anderson's staff had arrived to get the full story. To my surprise, Stern and Speer came to see me together, something they almost never did. Both men agreed that it was "front page" material and that a copy of the sworn affidavit that I was about to give to the Justice Department would probably cinch them breaking the story. The timing, they felt, would be excellent; Israel's Prime Minister Begin was scheduled to arrive in Washington in a few days. Both journalists said they would discuss the story with their respective bosses.

Things suddenly seemed to be moving very quickly. I rushed to the Justice Department to keep my 4:30 appointment with Civiletti. As I entered the impressive Justice building, I glanced up and saw the phrase, "Justice In The Life and Conduct of the State is Possible Only as First It Resides in the Heart and Souls of The Citizens," chiseled in stone. My heart pounded as I took the elevator to the fourth floor. I was about to give an eyewitness account of an incident involving a top-level Senate staffer; it was a major step toward "getting involved."

I arrived on time. The secretary led me to a back office where a tall, lean man in his early 60s was waiting. He introduced himself as John Davitt, Chief of the Justice Department's Internal Security Division. He spoke with some sort of speech impediment — a hoarse, gravelly voice with some stuttering — which might have been the result of an earlier operation.

I told him about the incident and asked if I had done the right thing by reporting it. He said yes, and explained that Bryen's actions could have several possible implications. For one, he might have been in violation of the Foreign Agents Registration Act, which requires those acting on behalf of another government to register with the Justice Department. A federal employee acting on behalf of another country is guilty of a crime because one cannot be a U.S. employee and a foreign agent at the same time, he said. Davitt quickly added that Bryen may only have been a good friend of the people with whom he met and may not have committed any legal violations.

Davitt described more serious possibilities. Any person who possesses classified documents and transmits them to

21

any person who is not authorized to receive them could be violating federal espionage laws. Davitt said he would take my information to the FBI Intelligence Division. The Division would check its files for any data on Bryen before deciding whether a full investigation would be conducted.

Everything that happened to me that day, the discussions and interviews with Abourezk, the reporters and the Justice Department's Internal Security Chief, heightened my belief that Bryen had betrayed his professional responsibilities and his country. The whirl of events seemed to lift me into the intriguing realm of international politics. "Espionage" was the term mentioned by Davitt. Could this be that serious?

I decided to stay in Washington for the next ten days and met with an attorney, Tom Shack, to prepare an affidavit recounting an official version of the Madison Hotel incident. By the following Monday, I submitted a 13-page affidavit to the Justice Department. I was invited by William Quandt, a Middle East specialist on the National Security Council, to come to the White House to review my affidavit with him. Quandt examined the affidavit and said that he believed such things were happening, but this was the first time he had seen evidence beyond heresay. He asked me if Morris Amitay, then head of the American-Israeli Public Affairs Committee, the major Israeli lobby organization, had been present at the Madison meeting. He was not, I replied. I would be asked this question again soon. Quandt said he would report the Bryen incident directly to Zbigniew Brzezinski. I thanked him and left.

It occurred to me that the two reporters with whom I had spoken the previous Friday had not gotten back in touch with me. They had been very excited about the story — and now not a word! Perhaps it was because Begin had postponed his visit to Washington as a result of Israel's invasion of Lebanon that weekend. I headed to Jack Anderson's office to give Speer a copy of the affidavit. Speer was supposed to be waiting for me, but was not there. The secretary, apparently confused, summoned Jack Anderson. Anderson appeared to be unfamiliar with the story, which surprised me because Speer had said he was going to discuss it with him. Anderson graciously took the affidavit and said he would look it over and get back to me. That was the last time I heard from him or his office.

The next day I spoke with Stern of the *Washington Post*. He reiterated his view that the story was of great interest and really should break big. But, he said, there was a "very attractive" young female reporter from the *Trenton Times* who wanted to interview me about the incident. He said that I probably would like to meet her because she was an "attractive woman." His attitude greatly concerned me. I was not a media expert, but I knew that reporters often jealously guard a story so they can break it first. Stern initially had told me this was front page material, and now he was actually trying to set me up with another reporter in New Jersey. Something was wrong.

Throughout the week, I repeatedly contacted Speer and Stern. They said that they were checking the details and would be breaking the story soon. Later, however, a Washington source called to tell me that neither would run the story. A friend then suggested I contact Nick Luddington of the Associated Press. Luddington and I met in the Madison Hotel, where I pointed out the tables at which Bryen, the Israelis and I were sitting. I gave him a copy of the affidavit. Somewhat tired and discouraged, I packed my bags and returned to North Dakota.

Two weeks later, Luddington called to let me know he was breaking the story on Saturday, April 1. He said that he had spoken with Bryen, who admitted meeting with the Israelis, but denied those portions of my affidavit describing irregularities on his part. He mentioned that a London-based Arab newspaper already had run the story. I did not know how the newspaper had learned of the story. I also received a call from Senator Abourezk, who told me that Adlai Stevenson, Chairman of the Select Committee on Standards and Conduct,* was interested in talking to me about the Madison Hotel incident and Stephen Bryen. When I returned to Washington in mid-April, however, I learned that Stevenson had dropped the issue.

On April 2, my uncle in Cedar Rapids, Iowa, called to tell me that the newspaper there had run a major story describing the Madison Hotel incident and my role in bringing it to light. It was Luddington's piece, which had gone over the AP wire to major newspapers. The story was picked up on the front page of the *Houston Post*, and by the *Atlanta Constitution* and the *Dallas Morning News*.

Luddington's article was well written and revealed a startling new fact: "A Defense Department official, who declined to be publicly identified, said that on March 8, the Pentagon sent to the Senate Foreign Relations Committee a classified analysis of the proposed U.S. sale of F-15 jets to Saudi Arabia . . . The report contained a description of Saudi air bases."[13]

But the story did not really focus first and foremost on whether Bryen had betrayed his duties by offering the Pentagon document to the Israelis. Rather, it led with this account: "In a hotel coffee shop, a Senate aide discusses the Middle East with four Israelis while a former lobbyist for an Arab-American group eavesdrops. The incident is perhaps typical of the growing contest for influence in the U.S. capital between newly active Arabs and the long-powerful Israeli lobby."[14]

The story discussed the incident in the context of President

---

*The Select Committee on Standards and Conduct was the forerunner to the Senate Select Committee on Ethics.

Carter's planned sale of F-15 jets to Egypt and the Saudis. It said that my allegations were being turned over to the FBI, but did not specify further.[15]

A few days later, the *Washington Post* finally ran an eight paragraph article, buried in one of the inside pages, reporting Bryen's sudden plans to take personal leave from his Committee job so he could "prepare for his upcoming wedding." The article noted in its lead that Bryen's decision to leave came after "accusations that he offered a Pentagon document on Arab military bases to Israeli officials." As in the AP story, Bryen denied offering the Pentagon document. Bryen was quoted as saying he had "suggested to the Israelis, in a discussion about Arabian bases that they ask for a briefing on the matter from the Pentagon."[16]

On April 6, the same day the *Post* article appeared, I received a call from FBI Agent Stephen Pletcher. He said he was working on the case and took me up on my offer to come to Washington and take a lie detector test. A week later I returned to Washington. My lawyer and I arrived at the FBI Washington field office to meet with Pletcher and take the exam. The examiner, who Pletcher said was the Bureau's finest and had just completed examining witnesses in the Tongsun Park Congressional bribery case, hooked me up to the machine and asked preliminary questions about my age and name. Then he concentrated on the incident and my affidavit.

"Have you concocted this story?" he asked.

"No," I answered.

"Have you ever committed a serious crime?"

"No."

"Did Stephen Bryen meet with the group at the Madison Hotel on March 9, 1978, to which you were party?"

"Yes."

"Did Stephen Bryen offer a Pentagon document to the

group at that time?"

"Yes."

"Is the affidavit true?"

"Yes."

"Have you ever lied to a public official?"

"No."

And that was it. Pletcher had his own questions. He asked me the name of the man with whom I was supposed to meet in the Madison Hotel that morning. [The man later told him of our appointment and confirmed that he had failed to show up.] Pletcher asked if Morris Amitay of AIPAC, the American-Israeli Public Affairs Committee, was present at the Madison Hotel meeting. He was not, I said, remembering that Quandt had asked the same question. Then Pletcher requested more details on items in my affidavit: the discussions of the West Bank, the Pentagon document, Erich von Marbod and "we-the-Israelis" versus "they-the-Americans." After going over these matters, Pletcher said it appeared I had passed the test. He would ask Bryen to take one, but there was a chance he would refuse.

Finally, Pletcher pulled me aside and warned me that I was likely to be followed by "the other side." He instructed that if anything strange happened I should call him immediately. He would be back in touch with me.

In two weeks Pletcher contacted my attorney to see if I would undergo hypnosis. The FBI used hypnosis in many cases to improve the recall abilities of potential witnesses. Pletcher indicated he was very interested in learning more about Bryen's references to "research and development" and in a description of those present at the table.

I told the FBI that I would undergo hypnosis, provided Shack, my attorney, and a psychiatrist I knew could be present, and that the session would be videotaped. Pletcher did not respond immediately to our proposed conditions. I decided to return to North Dakota and await a response from the FBI.

Months passed without a word from the FBI or any newspaper reporters. On August 14, a friend in Washington called to say that the Carter Administration somehow had used the Bryen incident as leverage in Congress to save the proposed sale of arms to Saudi Arabia and Egypt. He had heard that Stephen Bryen was going to appear before a grand jury. I then called Tom Shack in Washington, who said that as far as he knew, the investigation of Bryen was a "dead issue."

I was confused by this contradiction. One source, whom I knew well and trusted, said Bryen was going to appear before a grand jury. Yet my attorney had called the affair a "dead issue." I wanted to learn the truth, but the pull of my business affairs forced me to deal with the realities of making a living. The incident and ensuing events slowly slipped from my mind. I felt that I had done all that I could do.

On October 26, however, I learned that the Bryen investigation was far from dead. Pletcher surprised me with a call and told me he had left the FBI on June 1. That was news to me! I thought he had been handling the case all of the time. But he had left only one month after the last time I had spoken with him.

Pletcher said the man with whom I was supposed to meet in the Madison Hotel that morning had verified that he missed the appointment. He then told me that the FBI was moving ahead with the Bryen investigation and was upsetting a few people. It might go to a grand jury after the next session of Congress started, which would be in three months, he said. Meanwhile, an FBI agent named Tim Mahoney had taken his place and would be getting in touch with me for follow up questions. He wished me luck.

There are times in one's life when one looks back at a particular moment and asks, "Why didn't I say or do this differently?" This was one of those instances. Pletcher had caught me so far off guard with his call that I did not think quickly enough to ask a series of crucial questions that would nag me for years. After being so hot on Bryen's trail, why did Pletcher leave the FBI so suddenly? Why did he not follow up on the request to put me under hypnosis? Why in the world would they wait until Congress began the next session before forcing Bryen to appear before a grand jury? What did one have to do with the other?

And the investigation? What kind of relationship did Bryen have with the Israelis? Was the Madison incident the exception or the rule? If he did have cozy ties to the Israelis, was there additional evidence that he had played fast and loose with U.S. military secrets and compromised our security? Had others come forward and testified against Bryen?

Perhaps Pletcher would have refused to answer these questions. But I never got another chance to ask him. That was the last time we spoke.

It would be another five years before I even began getting answers to some of these questions. The search for answers became a quest demanding energies, resources and determination to expose the truth. Fortunately, others would join the quest and help to shed light on the Bryen case. The answers we found proved that we had a lot to worry about as Bryen himself moved on to bigger and better things.

CHAPTER 2

THE BRYEN-PERLE CONNECTION

Six weeks after I had spoken with FBI agent Pletcher about the investigation, Tim Mahoney, the FBI agent who had taken charge of the Bryen investigation, called me. He repeated the usual questions about the interview notes, Bryen's offering of the Pentagon document and my willingness to undergo hypnosis. I went over each subject with him and reminded him that my attorney had proposed conditions for hypnosis and that we were awaiting the FBI's response. Mahoney seemed as eager as Pletcher to dig into the case. He said that he expected to wrap it up in no more than two months.

I wondered why the investigation had dragged on for so long. Nine months had passed since I reported Bryen's actions to the Justice Department. Two seemingly top flight agents had worked on the case. But the first quietly left the Bureau and the second took six months to contact me — and then asked the same questions that were posed when the whole thing started!

By mid-January, however, it appeared the FBI's work was having some impact and that I might get the answers to my questions about Bryen and the investigation. A journalist in Washington called to say that Bryen was expected to leave his Senate Foreign Relations Committee job within weeks. "Leave his job?" I asked. "I thought he left last April!"

The caller explained that Bryen had returned in November

29

1978, to finish up work for Senator Clifford Case in the wake of his election defeat to a primary challenger. Case, a New Jersey Republican who became the ranking minority member of the Senate Foreign Relations Committee, had initially hired Bryen in 1971 to work on his personal staff. Case later shifted Bryen to a spot on the Senate Foreign Relations Committee.

I soon learned that the journalist was correct: Bryen left his job on February 9, 1979, to take a job with the Coalition for a Democratic Majority. Somehow this seemed an odd move. Why would Bryen, a seven-year employee of a Republican Senator, go to work for a bunch of Democrats? It was an important question. In seeking the answer, I discovered that I could no longer think of Bryen as a pro-Zionist lone ranger fighting a covert crusade. Rather, I became acquainted with a whole new cast of characters whose relationships with one another were often complex as well as intriguing. Initially, the process diverted my attention away from Bryen himself. As the search continued, however, I discovered an intricate network of influential people whose policies meshed with Bryen's and who more often than not had some direct or indirect professional or personal relationship with him.

The Coalition for a Democratic Majority was founded in 1973 by Senator Henry Jackson, Daniel Patrick Moynihan and other hawkish Democrats who were determined to battle the "McGovern wing" of the party and advocate tougher policies on defense and national security issues. It was an organization whose membership was only letter head deep, but the members were heavyweights. Ben Wattenberg, for instance, was a renowned expert on electoral politics, an author and columnist. Jeanne Kirkpatrick was a professor at Georgetown University and later became President Reagan's Ambassador to the United Nations — a post Moynihan held previously. Myer Rashish assumed the post as Undersecretary of State for Economic Affairs in the Reagan Administration. Elliot

Abrams, another prominent Coalition member, joined the Reagan State Department as Assistant Secretary for Human Rights. Norman Podhoretz was a noted author and "former liberal." Throughout the 1970s, these Coalition members emerged as leading voices for larger defense budgets, and a "hard-line" stance against the Soviets.

By joining the Coalition, Bryen had moved into a powerful circle. It was not immediately clear, however, how Bryen's move jibed with his strong pro-Israel thinking. Then one day I found a new book by Norman Podhoretz, entitled *Breaking Ranks*, which helped to shed some light on Bryen's affinity with the Coalition. Editor of *Commentary* magazine* since 1960, Podhoretz once had been a leading advocate of liberal political views. By the early 1970's, however, he had become disenchanted with the orthodox liberals who favored cuts in military spending and less American interventionism abroad.

In *Breaking Ranks*, Podhoretz described the evolution of his political thought, the founding of the Coalition and the relationship between a strong United States military machine and the future of Israel. Citing the Soviet-backed Egyptian surprise attack on Israel that set off the 1973 war, Podhoretz wrote, "What had saved Israel from being overrun by the Arab armies was an airlift of American arms; and what had prevented the Russians from intervening when they threatened to do so at a certain point was the American nuclear deterrent. Nothing could have more vividly demonstrated the inextricable connection between the survival of Israel and the military adequacy of the United States."[1]

Podhoretz continued, "The inextricable connection between the survival of Israel and American military strength was an

---

Commentary is published by the New York office of the American Jewish Committee.

idea I soon also had the opportunity to lend support to during Pat Moynihan's race against Bella Abzug and Ramsey Clark for the Democratic nomination for the United States Senate in New York in 1976. He countered the calls of Abzug and Clark for deep cuts in military spending with the argument that a society worth defending also needed to be defended by an adequate military budget. It was in the course of raising this issue that Moynihan was able to demonstrate more vividly than anyone had done before that there was a direct contradiction between caring about the survival of Israel — as both Abzug and Clark professed to — and opposing, as they both did, the defense appropriations out of which aid to Israel had to come."[2]

The words hit me like a bucket of cold water. Podhoretz had outlined the philosophical connections between pro-Israel policies, on the one hand, and increased military spending made rational and acceptable by anti-Soviet rhetoric on the other. By equating "Arabs and the Russians — and those Americans sunk in the 'patterns of appeasement',"[3] he had set forth a political philosophy which was embraced by those who wanted to shape American foreign and military policy according to the interests of Israel.

Podhoretz's views were in part revealed by the Coalition which he helped to found, a coalition which was willing to employ someone who was being investigated by the FBI for possible violations of United States espionage laws. A closer look at another of the Coalition's founders, Senator Henry Jackson, was even more revealing. I remembered how Bryen, in his Madison Hotel meeting with the Israelis, kept referring to Jackson as if they were close friends. In fact, Bryen had very close connections with Jackson's office, mainly because he was a close friend of Jackson's most active staffer, Richard Perle.

Several reporters who contacted me about the Bryen case advised me that Bryen and Perle were ideological soulmates.

Perle was said to be a quintessential Senate staffer: hard working, well-connected and adroit with the press corps. He was right out of the Podhoretz mold, calling for increased military spending, ardent support of Israel, and a hard-line against the Soviets. Perle had emerged as the key staffer fighting the Carter Administration on the SALT II treaty negotiations with the Soviets. In the past he had authored the Jackson amendment, which was supposed to help Soviet Jews by withholding "most favored nation" status from Socialist countries that restricted emigration rights. He had helped write a law to strengthen curbs on export technology to the Soviet bloc. Perle was also known as an infamous leaker of information to the Evans and Novak syndicated column. As one member of Congress said, "I can't tell you the number of things Perle has told me that a few days later showed up in Evans and Novak."[4]

Shortly after being told about the Perle-Bryen connection, I learned of a *New York Times* article which reported that CIA Director Stansfield Turner had fired a senior CIA analyst for leaking top secret material on Soviet missile strength to Perle. The November 13, 1978, story reported that David S. Sullivan, the CIA analyst, had given Perle a memo which he had authored which claimed that the Soviets were deceiving the United States on its missile strength and were surpassing us in military might. Sullivan turned over the material to Perle so that Senator Jackson could use it in the fight against ratification of the SALT treaty.[5]

Turner was "outraged" by Sullivan's insubordination, "as well as the decision of Senator Jackson and Mr. Perle, who have high security clearances, to receive the working level documents. The Sullivan materials included some of the Government's most closely held information on sources and methods of obtaining information about the Soviet Union," the *Times* reported.[6]

After firing Sullivan, Turner met twice with Jackson and urged him to fire Perle. "That's what we did on our end, and that's what you should do on your end," Turner told Jackson. Although Jackson and Perle apologized to Turner and returned the documents to the CIA, no further action was taken. In his *New York Times* article, Seymour Hersch concluded, "The CIA perhaps could have taken more severe sanctions against Mr. Sullivan, the official added, but to do more, they'd have to take on Jackson and they were afraid to do it."[7]

Several years later, in his book on Henry Kissinger, Seymour Hersch unveiled another incident in which Perle had been caught divulging classified data. This incident had involved the Israelis. In his discussion on the wiretapping of Kissinger aide Hal Sonnenfeldt, Hersch wrote, "The . . . document in question . . . was an FBI summary of a wiretap on the Israeli Embassy in which Richard N. Perle, an aide to Senator Henry Jackson, was overheard discussing classified information that had been supplied to him by someone on the National Security Council . . . (Kissinger) forwarded the material to (H.R.) Haldeman, who immediately telephoned (J. Edgar) Hoover, according to FBI documents, and ordered the FBI be assigned to determine which NSC staffer was in contact with Richard Perle."[8]

"In a telephone call on October 15, 1970, to Hoover, Haldeman invoked the name of Henry Kissinger in asking for another wiretap of Sonnenfeldt. Kissinger had to realize that Haldeman and Hoover would suspect Sonnenfeldt, who was known from previous wiretaps to have close ties to the Israelis as well as to Perle. Sonnenfeldt, a former State Department intelligence official, had been repeatedly investigated by the FBI for other suspected leaks early in his career."[9]

As I continued looking into Perle's background, I was alerted to a curious incident which took place in April 1976. Nelson Rockefeller, then Vice-President to Gerald Ford, implied in a meeting with Georgia Republicans that one member of Senator Henry Jackson's staff was a "Communist," and that another had a "questionable background." The remarks were directed at Jackson staffers Dorothy Fosdick and Richard Perle.[10] The media jumped on the story as Jackson and other Senators accused Rockefeller of "McCarthyism," and demanded an apology. Rockefeller reluctantly apologized. But as the *Economist* magazine reported, "The vice president tried to foster the same rumor in January, at an editorial conference held by *Time* magazine . . . Just what provoked this depressing episode remains obscure. The vice president is sticking by his vague and generalized belief that unfriendly foreigners are making use of the 'political system' for deleterious ends."[11] No one ever found out what specifically had prompted Rockefeller's repeated attempts to smear Perle.

It was clear that Perle shared Bryen's extremely pro-Israel views, but for the next year I was so consumed with business projects, traveling and other matters that I lost track of both Perle and Bryen.

Early in 1980, however, I returned to Washington and learned that Bryen had become the Executive Director of an organization called the Jewish Institute for National Security Affairs. Known as JINSA, the group was dedicated to "communicating" the need for greater American military support for Israel.

News of Bryen's venture fell like a dark shadow across my consciousness, as I virtually had forgotten about the FBI investigation. I kicked myself for not staying on top of the case. Something must have gone wrong. Mahoney, the FBI agent, had made it sound like they would be taking some action against Bryen. But that had been almost two years earlier. Since then there had been no announcements from the Justice Department. The press had lost interest.

Once again, I felt compelled to find out what had happened

with the FBI's investigation. When the case was opened, my interviews with John Davitt, Pletcher and Mahoney convinced me that the U.S. Government was on the side of those who wanted to expose Bryen. But my renewed search for answers would soon reveal that the Government had changed sides. It no longer wanted to shed light on Bryen or its own role in investigating him. Was a cover up about to begin?

CHAPTER 3

CRACKS IN THE STONEWALL: THE FOIA REQUEST

The Justice Department, like all law enforcement agencies, generally refuses to comment publicly on a pending investigation. The "no comment" policy is intended to protect innocent people from adverse publicity before an investigation is closed and formal action taken. It also is supposed to avoid the risk of jeopardizing the Government's case against a potential suspect by airing charges in the press and possibly prejudicing a future jury. The little I learned about the Bryen investigation from FBI agents Stephen Pletcher and Tim Mahoney was possible because I was a witness with whom they had had direct, albeit brief, contact.

A few of the journalists who delved into the case had mentioned to me that the investigation appeared to expand well beyond the initial allegations. They were under the impression that investigators had started to compile a file on Bryen. Most of the newsmen, however, had become frustrated in their efforts to learn more about the file or to confirm any of the rumors they had heard.

I became more and more curious about whether such a file existed and more importantly, what was in it. A few friends and trusted colleagues said the best way to find out about the Justice Department file was through the U.S. Freedom of Information Act [FOIA]. The law requires federal agencies to identify and disclose certain records to individuals who requested them in writing.

Cherif Bassiouni, professor of Law at DePaul University in Chicago, told me the FOIA had enabled him to expose an FBI spy program called "Operation Boulder." Under the program, the FBI in Colorado scanned various lists of people and singled out those with Arabic surnames as targets for a sweeping "terrorist" investigation. According to documents Bassiouni obtained after a lengthy legal battle, the spy project was based on the incredible, racist notion that all Arabs were potential terrorists.

There were other examples. The American Palestine Committee had been able to get Central Intelligence Agency documents indicating that Israeli Foreign Minister Moshe Dayan deliberately ordered an attack on the U.S. Navy ship *Liberty* during the 1967 War. The American Jewish Congress had forced the Commerce Department to release details about efforts by Arab countries to get U.S. companies to boycott Israel. Journalists had learned about illegal surveillance of Martin Luther King, Jr., Felix Frankfurter, Helen Keller, Clarence Darrow and scores of prominent, law abiding Americans. The record was clear: the FOIA had helped alert the public to the actions of governmental agencies by providing freer access to information.[1]

A serious effort to get the file, however, would entail a lot of time and legal expenses. I was in no position to retain a lawyer for an extended period, and although I did not want the Bryen affair to become an Arab-Israeli conflict, I felt that the National Association of Arab Americans was the only group which would be willing and financially able to assist me with an FOIA request. On a brief visit to Washington, I discussed the idea with J.R. AbiNader, then Executive Director of the NAAA. AbiNader agreed that the FOIA approach would be the best way to force the Justice Department to turn over its records on Bryen. It would also renew press attention to the case. The NAAA Board approved the move.

The NAAA sent the FOIA request to the Justice Department in April 1980. The first communication from the Department was dated 6 August 1980 and read:

> This is in reference to your letter requesting records pursuant to the Freedom of Information Act, pertaining to an investigation into allegations that Stephen Bryen may have violated espionage laws.
>
> We have located index references to the files which contain the records you seek. We estimate that the files consist of 600 pages for which we will charge you a reproduction fee of $60.00 (10 cents per page).
>
> However, no remittance should be made at this time. Because of the volume of requests received by the Criminal Division we have acquired a substantial backlog of requests, which like yours, will require the examination of records. In order to be fair to all requestors, we are completing requests in the order in which they were received in proper form (i.e., in the case of Freedom of Information request, when the records requested have been reasonably described.)
>
> There are 83 requests preceding yours on our list of Freedom of Information Act requests requiring the examination of records. Please be assured that we are exercising all possible diligence, given the volume of requests and personnel limitations, to process requests received by us as rapidly as possible. We will process your request as soon as we have completed those received prior to yours. When we near your request, we will inform you, at which time an advance deposit of 25% of the estimated search fee should be remitted.

If you feel that exigent or unique circumstances exist which warrant that your request ought to be taken out of order and processed ahead of other requests, please communicate the nature of the circumstances to us. We will, if the circumstances warrant, make every effort to expedite such a request.[2]

Clearly, we were on to something big. The fact that there was a 600-page file on Bryen indicated that the FBI had conducted a major investigation. I read the letter again. It was signed by E. Ross Buckley, Chief of the Criminal Division's Freedom of Information/Privacy Act Unit. The letter did not say precisely when the documents would be released. It seemed reasonable, however, that they would work on a "first-come, first-serve" basis.

The fact that the Department had compiled a file of 600 pages certainly helped to explain why Bryen had left his Senate job and had ended up with a group that specialized in the relationship between American and Israeli security needs. The Jewish Institute for National Security Affairs began as a study group in 1976 and became fully operational in December, 1979, when Bryen was named Executive Director and editor of its newsletter.

In a 1979 newsletter article entitled "The Link Between Israel and the United States: JINSA's Purpose," the group explained what it was all about:

When a group of us came together three years ago to found the Jewish Institute for Natinal(sic) Security Affairs, we were concerned about the need to inform the Jewish community of the importance of American defense to the survival of Israel. We also thought it important to educate the American public on the geopolitical values of Israel to the United States as an outpost of Western interests in the Middle East . . .

More than ever before, the interests of the United States and Israel are intertwined. Israel is not likely to survive in a Soviet-dominated Middle East in which extremists are given free rein. At the same time, a Soviet-dominated Middle East would end the role of the United States as a major world power and would cripple the American economy. It follows that the watchword of the Israeli defense forces "ein breira" ("there is no alternative") holds good for both Israel and the United States, in what should be their joint effort to block moves in the Middle East by the Soviet Union and its proxies, including the PLO.

While our basic propositions that the United States must strengthen its conventional military capability, that the lifeline to the Persian Gulf must be secured, that Israel already plays (and must play in the future) an important role in securing that lifeline, are generally accepted now, it is still an open question whether these accepted propositions are being acted on.

Sometime ago, it was announced that a United States Middle East "Strike Force" or Quick Reaction Force would be created to intervene in situations in which the free world oil supply from the Middle East was threatened by a hostile takeover. It is reported today that this force is far from assembled — it remains by and large a planner's concept. The military admits freely that the transport to move the force, to the Middle East or elsewhere, may be insufficient. There is a gap in our defensive structure that needs to be bridged.

There are many other questions of concern. Is the United States Sixth Fleet in the Mediterranean equipped adequately to guard America's interests in the region? Do we need a Fifth Fleet in the Indian Ocean to guard against growing Soviet strength there, and, if we do, how can one be developed? Do we need to take advantage of Israel's Etzion base in the Sinai, near Elat, which is regarded as one of the best equipped bases in the world but scheduled for demilitarization by the Camp David agreements? Would it not be in the best interests of all countries in the region, and the Western world generally, for Etzion to remain a military base, operated by the United States?

One of the reasons America is regarded highly in the Middle East and Persian Gulf is because Israel is perceived as a strong force for stability in the region. But Israel alone is not enough — America's prestige and capability has been declining and this invites armed conflicts and revolution from within. Critical resources, as those in Saudi Arabia, are under threat.

What steps can and should be taken to protect America's interest in the Middle East? It is to these and related questions that the coming issues of the JINSA Newsletter will be devoted.[3]

The Jewish Institute for National Security Affairs went beyond the philosophical support of the Coalition for a Democratic Majority for pro-Israel militarism coupled with anti-Soviet defense policies. It was set up to monitor current events and voice the proper policy, issue by issue, needed to strengthen the strategic bond between the United States and Israel. JINSA did not agree with various U.S. Administrations who believed that American foreign policy interests required improved relations with Arab nations and consideration of the Palestinian problem. The JINSA line was simple: what was good for Israel was good for America. There was "no alternative," they claimed.

JINSA's founders included Max M. Kampelman, who became co-chairman of the U.S. delegation to the Conference on Security and Cooperation in Europe in 1981, and Richard Schifter, a U.S. representative to the United Nations in 1981. Its Board of Directors included Michael Ledeen, an expert on identifying "who's who" in international experts, Saul Stern, and Morris J. Amitay, former head of the American-Israeli Public Affairs Committee. Senator Rudy Boschwitz (R-Mn) and Eugene V. Rostow of the Reagan Administration's Arms Control and Disarmament Agency joined the Board of Advisors. Frank Hoeber, whose wife was the principal Deputy Assistant Secretary of the Army for Research, Development and Acquisition, became a contributing editor of the JINSA newsletter.

The JINSA newsletter covered a broad spectrum of issues from an unabashedly militaristic point of view. Moreover, the newsletter tied U.S. interests world-wide to U.S. support of Israel and Israel's own interests. For example, in an April 1980 article entitled "Red Clouds over the Caribbean," JINSA focused on the takeover of Grenada by the Marxist Maurice Bishop and warned that a Marxist Grenada "could become a base for Soviet operations." But in addition to warning against the Marxist takeover of the Caribbean island, the article stressed that Bishop supported an independent Palestinian state and that he denounced "repeated Zionist attacks against Lebanon." The article went on to criticize the Carter Administration for not devising a suitable policy to deal with the threats posed by what it called the "Soviet and radical-Arab drive" in Latin America. "Such a policy," the article concluded, "is badly needed for our own defense as well as our role as peacemaker in the Middle East."[4]

According to JINSA's line of reasoning, Maurice Bishop's support of a Palestinian state was a threat to U.S. security and the U.S. role in the Middle East. While a Marxist Grenada may have posed a threat to U.S. interests, what did Bishop's attitude toward the Palestinians have to do with our national security? By tying the Soviets to Grenada, and Grenada to the PLO, JINSA tied being against Soviet adventurism in Latin America to being anti-PLO, pro-strong Israel. Not to support a militarily strong Israel to counter this "radical-Arab threat" was to support Soviet aggression and terrorism, according to JINSA's argument.

This view surfaced again in an editorial on PLO Chairman Yaser Arafat's visit to Nicaragua to meet with Salvadorean guerrilla leaders. The editorial stated, "clearly, the PLO shifts from a troublesome and obstreperous revolutionary organization with which we must come to terms — to an adversary of American interests . . . Among the implications for the United States is the requirement that if we want to protect and preserve pro-American governments such as the Government of El Salvador, we have to choke off the supply of weapons and training of the revolutionaries at the source. There is a variety of 'sources' to contend with — and one surely is the Palestine Liberation Organization."[5]

Without examining U.S. policy in El Salvador, JINSA called for alteration of U.S. policy toward the Palestinians because of Arafat's meeting with the Salvadorean guerrillas. Once again, U.S. concerns in Latin America were tied to the Middle East. By emphasizing what it regarded as a Soviet - Salvadorean guerrilla - PLO contact, JINSA called for an American policy which advocated a strong Israel to contend with the "Palestinian threat." By tying the PLO to revolutionaries against a pro-American government, Israel's foes became America's foes.

Other articles stressed the need to increase the defense budget so that the United States would have more nuclear missiles, battleships, fighter jets and military personnel. JINSA blamed the so-called "Vietnam Syndrome" and the

Carter Administration for neglecting the defense budget.[6] It wanted to put more money into defense, and did not seem to consider the consequences of increased defense appropriations for the U.S. economy.

While JINSA's articles covered many subjects, one central theme emerged from its editorials: the need for a U.S. military presence in the Middle East. For nearly two decades, U.S. Administrations had been reluctant to take on a permanent Middle East role out of fear that it would lead to a no-win involvement in the strife-torn region. In more recent years, the United States had attempted to broker peace between Israelis and Arabs. U.S. leaders understood that a direct military presence would jeopardize those efforts.

JINSA, however, claimed that by working with Israel, the United States could establish the equivalent of a base at a much lower cost. "Israel has extraordinarily good facilities and excellent technicians trained to handle U.S. equipment of the most modern kind," it said in one editorial. "Money is saved because we do not have to spend millions on costly repair equipment or send technicians and specialists en masse 6,000 miles from home. We do not have to build storage depots, or train men to guard installations and keep them well run. All of that is already there. What we need to do is supplement the facilities already on the ground, and work out specific agreements covering use. We should, of course, not expect any of this for free."[7]

An editorial on the proposed sale of AWACS to the Saudis advocated a "package deal" to give "America a realistic option to retrieve the systems in case of the chance of compromise to it. Such an approach might work in two steps," it said. "STEP ONE: just as AWACS is presently on loan to Saudi Arabia, apparently until 1985, although it is being manned and operated principally by the United States, so too should the U.S. put on loan interceptor aircraft which will be manned principally by the United States. STEP TWO: To protect and balance the post-1985 environment, America needs a physical presence in a base either on Israeli territory, or, alternatively, at Etzion or Etam in the Sinai."[8]

Another editorial discussed the Pentagon's "Gallant Knight" project, which was designed to move a U.S. Rapid Deployment Force into a position which would blunt any possible Soviet invasion of Iran. While a larger defense budget would enhance such a force, the editorial added that "Saudi Arabia has to re-evaluate its stand on U.S. bases in the Middle East before scenarios such as 'Gallant Knight' can be anything other than 'Disneyland in the Mock Desert'."[9]

In a separate editorial, JINSA endorsed the idea of "compensating" Israel for the sale of additional equipment for F-15 fighter jets to the Saudis. "But when we speak about compensation, America must also be concerned about compensating itself," it continued. "In looking at U.S. policy in the Middle East and Persian Gulf, America has to build relations that assure our ability to respond to a crisis in the area. In this regard, our self-compensation ought to be aimed at gaining facilities, installations and assets in the area that can help us. Specific arrangements with Israel, as with other countries, ought to be extremely high on our agenda."[10]

The JINSA job provided Bryen with the opportunity to openly advocate pro-Israeli policies without the usual constraints that encumber a Senate staff position. He took advantage of the opportunity by seizing a variety of separate issues to push for a U.S. military presence in the Middle East. It did not matter what was involved — a possible oil crisis, the need for a more capable Rapid Deployment Force, or jets to the Saudis — Bryen's answer was the same: put U.S. troops somewhere near Israeli soil, or at least set up strategic cooperation so American weapons and facilities are in place with the Israelis acting as our keepers.

As editor, Bryen also was able to go public with arguments he undoubtedly had made behind the scenes while he was in the Senate. A 4,000 word article argued against United States plans to sell additional spare parts for F-15 fighters to the Saudis. According to the article, the spare parts would enable the jets to strike well beyond Saudi borders, and would affect the balance of power. "Saudi Arabia can attack Israel, for example, without mustering her aircraft at a base close to Israel's territory. Instead, she can operate from distant bases beyond the eyes and ears of Israel's early warning network. There is, therefore, no doubt that Israel is negatively affected if Saudi Arabia actually gets the extra equipment."[11]

The article noted that several foreign policy experts felt the relatively minimal risk to Israel was outweighed by the United States' need to improve relations with Saudi Arabia. But JINSA challenged this view and said America should focus on the Saudis' connections with the Soviets. It cited Saudi support for the Palestine Liberation Organization and Iraq, which, it said, were two Soviet surrogates which promote international terrorism. Moreover, it charged, "Saudi Arabia is not helping the United States in its effort to build a presence in the region. To the contrary, Saudi Arabia officially opposes any U.S. presence — in particular, it has no intention of giving the U.S. access to bases on its own soil. In addition, despite clear recognition by the United States of Israel as an important strategic asset, Saudi Arabia is mustering its considerable resources to break that relationship."[12]

"Saudi Arabia has opened its ports to Soviet and Eastern European flag vessels carrying Russian-made arms, including 100 modern battle tanks, bound for Iraq. This arrangement implies that the Soviets and Bloc countries are doing business with Saudi Arabia. This presents problems for the United States that cannot be wished away."[13]

The articles in the JINSA newsletter intensified my impressions of Bryen. As I became more familiar with his writing, I realized Bryen's role was more profound than I had originally thought. He was more than a collector of valuable data for the Israelis. He appeared to be a major strategist who constantly sought the means and rationale to align American and Israeli defense policies.

The JINSA article on the F-15 sale clearly showed that a major part of Bryen's strategy was equating, as Podhoretz had done, Arabs and Soviets. By depicting Arab states as tools of the Soviets, the bond between Israel and the United States would be strengthened. Put simply, Israel's enemies would become America's enemies. But Bryen had to use tortured logic to advance this argument. For example, he said that since the Saudis had friendly relations with the PLO and Iraq, who, in turn, were friends of the Soviet Union, the United States could not trust the Saudis. Bryen did not discuss Saudi Arabia's own strategic interests in its relations with Iraq during the Iranian War, or whether international political considerations affected its policy toward the PLO. Nor did he mention that Saudi Arabia is one of the few nations which does not have diplomatic relations with the Soviet Union. Instead, he advocated a simplistic form of nationalistic "guilt by association" as the main determinant of U.S. foreign policy. Bryen's strategy, rooted in Israeli fear of its neighbors, carried frightening implications for the United States, for it sought to couple America with Israel in a regional isolation that would only jeopardize U.S. efforts to bring about a lasting peace in the Middle East.

The article on the F-15 sales reminded me of Bryen's Madison Hotel meeting, but it put the incident in a different light. The FBI and the press naturally were preoccupied with the possibility that Bryen had breached espionage laws by offering the document. But the main purpose of the session appears to have been to permit Bryen to advise the Israelis on which strategies to pursue in order to secure American support in several different areas.

He bluntly told them the sale of jets to Egypt could not be stopped, but said that perhaps the sale to the Saudis could be altered.* He also advised the Israelis to make good use of their research and development so as to build their own jets. With respect to buying fighters from the United States in the meantime, he said, "we can make them bargain." I wondered if this related to the package deal later worked out in Congress that sent jets to Israel, Egypt and the Saudis.

Bryen's strategy for securing Israel's hold on the West Bank — emphasizing security needs rather than religious and historical claims — was followed by Israeli defense officials and supporters in Congress.

The strategy was well-conceived. Bryen knew the Israelis had no intentions of lifting their hold on the West Bank. He also knew they needed to garner substantial Congressional support to counter President Carter's efforts to negotiate a withdrawal. But Bryen realized it would be too much to ask Congressional leaders to defend the Israelis' actions on the dubious religious and historical grounds espoused by Begin. The security claims were much more palatable on Capitol Hill, and fit in with Bryen's master strategy of uniting Israel and America in the ongoing fight against PLO "terrorism," which Bryen viewed as an outgrowth of Soviet imperialism.

Although I could not agree with Bryen's policy of tying the U.S. to Israel's interests, at least Bryen was now pursuing these policies through JINSA and not the Senate Foreign Relations Committee. If Bryen had indeed betrayed his country while working for the Senate, the FBI was taking care

---

*The sale to the Saudis was not altered, however, partly because the FBI investigation of Bryen took him out of the picture for a while.

of it, and I would find out more about that when the Justice Department disclosed the file. And even if Bryen was leading a group advocating closer military ties between Israel and the United States, he was, after all, only exercising his First Amendment rights — the same rights which permitted me to speak out against those policies. At least now the American taxpayers were no longer paying for it.

Richard Perle also left his Senate job and formed a consulting firm called the Abington Corporation, which specialized in defense and security issues. Perle formed the firm with John Lehman, another hard-liner who had been with the U.S. Arms Control Disarmament Agency.* I wondered if Perle and Bryen would enjoy private life enough to stay there, and then fade from the public policy arena.

---

*John Lehman later became Secretary of the Navy in the Administration of Ronald Reagan.

CHAPTER 4

FRIENDS IN HIGH PLACES

The Presidential campaign of 1980 was dominated by defense issues, as well as by developments in the Middle East. Ronald Reagan vowed that the bolstering of America's military strength, which he said had been declining since the end of the Vietnam War, would be a top priority for his Administration. Reagan said increased defense spending was needed to counter the growing Soviet threat worldwide.

His views were well-timed and struck a chord with American voters. The country was frustrated by President Carter's inability to free the American hostages in Iran. Nightly newscasts showing fanatics burning the American flag in the streets of Tehran brought a sense of humiliation for many. The botched rescue mission, in which U.S. helicopters burned in the Iranian desert, added to that sentiment.

Soviet adventurism was on the rise. The Soviet army had invaded Afghanistan and positioned 80,000 troops within striking distance of the Iranian border and, more importantly, near the oil-rich Gulf which borders Iran and Saudi Arabia. The Soviet influence was also growing in Nicaragua following the overthrow of the Somoza government.

Reagan drove home the point time and again: America could not be secure in such a volatile world unless it returned to its status as a military power second to none.

On election day in November 1980, the public's dissatisfaction with Carter came through loud and clear: Ronald Reagan was elected President. Although the Reagan romp was not predicted, and no one could be quite sure whether the victory represented more of an anti-Carter than a pro-Reagan vote, political pundits immediately seized upon the results to pronounce a tidal wave of change in American sentiments. The American people had become more conservative, they said. The Reagan victory marked the end of the Democrats' era of New Deal-style coalitions and the beginning of a conservative coalition. The welfare state was in trouble; the Pentagon was headed for better times. Americans wanted "big government" to take two steps backwards, and they were more interested in guns than butter, the experts said.

As I watched the election returns come in, I thought about Podhoretz's preachings on the need for a bigger defense budget, a tougher stance on the Soviets, and a strong pro-Israel Middle East policy. I recalled how Bryen advocated the same policies. Both wanted the United States to be not only ready but also willing to intervene militarily wherever a threat arose.

Despite efforts by his campaign team to make him appear as moderate as possible, it was plain that Ronald Reagan's view on defense paralleled those of Podhoretz and Bryen. Moreover, Reagan had made it clear he considered the Russians to be the root of much evil in the world. He planned to "talk tough" to them, and he would seek the defense resources necessary to back up his words.

Reagan had criticized Carter for stating that he would use arms to prevent any Soviet move in the Gulf area because, he said, the United States lacked the force to do so. In an interview given shortly after taking office, he virtually endorsed the strategy Bryen had been pushing. "What I have called for, and what I think is needed as we refurbish our capability, is a presence in the Middle East," Reagan said. "Not

the stationing of troops that could stop the Soviet Union if
they set out to advance logistically; we know that we couldn't
do that. What is meant by a presence is that we're there
enough to know and for the Soviets to know that if they made
a reckless move, they would be risking a confrontation with
the United States."[1]

On the issue of Israelis on the West Bank, Reagan said, "I
disagreed when the previous Administration referred to them
as illegal, they're not illegal. Not under the U.N. resolution
that leaves the West Bank open to all people — Arab and
Israeli alike, Christian alike. I do think perhaps now with this
rush to do it and this moving in there the way they [Israelis]
are is ill-advised because if we're going to continue with the
spirit of Camp David and try and arrive at peace, maybe, at
this time, is unnecessarily provocative."[2]

Reagan held that America had a moral commitment to
Israel's right to continue living as a nation. He added, "I think
that Israel, being a country sharing our same ideals, I think
democratic approach to things, with a combat-ready and even
a combat-experienced military, is a force in the Middle East
that is actually of benefit to us."[3]

Reagan said that the United States "morally should do
everything it can, in an even-handed manner, to bring peace
to the Middle East." A major hurdle, he added, was the refusal
of some Arab states to accept Israel's right to exist. "peace will
come when that first step is taken . . . . But again, it starts with
the acceptance of Israel as a nation."

Since Reagan also referred to the Camp David accords as the
"first step" towards peace in the Middle East, some optimis-
tically speculated that his Administration might eventually
expand the peace process.[4]

But it was not long before the news came that dashed hopes
of an even-handed Middle East policy. A man who claimed to
work in the Pentagon, but who would not identify himself,

called the National Association of Arab Americans to warn them that Stephen Bryen already was working in the Pentagon as a consultant to Richard Perle* and soon would be appointed Deputy Assistant Secretary of Defense for International Security Policy. Remembering that Bryen had been the subject of an FBI espionage investigation, the anonymous caller urged the NAAA to look into the matter.

Within two weeks he called again to ask why the NAAA had not gotten Bryen removed from the Pentagon. "This is serious," the anonymous caller said, "his papers are in to make him permanent."

I called David Sadd, who had taken over as Executive Director of NAAA, to get the full story and see if there was anything we could do about the Bryen appointment. Sadd agreed that NAAA would have to take action and said that they had already begun to reactivate the FOIA request. First, it would try to get the Justice Department to speed up its processing of the FOIA request. He said NAAA had not heard a peep out of the Justice Department since nine months ago when it said the group was 83rd on the list.

Second, NAAA might consider raising questions about the nominations. Although Bryen could take a Deputy Assistant Secretary job without being confirmed, Perle would be subject to a full confirmation hearing before the Senate Armed Services Committee. Perhaps NAAA could use the Perle hearings to challenge the appointment of Bryen. Sadd said he would discuss these ideas with the NAAA Board.

The prospect of seeing Bryen in a high-level Defense Department position galvanized the NAAA Board. What had been a rather hesitant group a year earlier when the FOIA request was first proposed was now unified and ready to take

---

*Richard Perle was appointed Assistant Secretary of Defense for International Security Policy and appointed Bryen to be his Deputy Assistant Secretary.

action. The Board agreed that something would have to be done to expedite disclosure of the Bryen file, and that it would consider hiring an attorney specializing in the FOIA. In the meantime, it would do as much as possible to alert the Congress, the White House and the Defense Department to the security risk that Bryen posed. The main goal was to get the Senate to review the Bryen file and hopefully persuade Perle to drop Bryen's appointment.

The NAAA soon found out it had no chance of getting the Bryen file from the Justice Department in time for Perle's July confirmation hearing before the Senate Armed Services Committee. The day of the hearing, the NAAA sent letters to Congressional leaders, White House aides and the Defense Department. Typical of the correspondence was a two-page letter from Sadd to Senator Edward Zorinsky, of the Senate Armed Services Committee, which was accompanied by a copy of my 1978 affidavit describing the Madison Hotel incident.

We believe the following material may be of interest to you regarding the confirmation hearings of Mr. Richard Perle as Assistant Secretary of Defense for International Security Policy. The material contains information concerning allegations that Stephen Bryen, presently a consultant for Mr. Perle at the Department of Defense, may have violated U.S. espionage laws by offering sensitive documents to Israeli government officials in the spring of 1978.

We believe this information is important. We do not question Mr. Perle's technical proficiency. Rather, we have sincere concerns about his judgment and motivation in appointing to a sensitive position a man about whom there are unanswered questions related to alleged violations of U.S. espionage laws.

We hope that by bringing this matter to your attention you will be able to satisfy your concerns that the Senate Armed Services Committee will not confirm to a sensitive position a man who has displayed staff preferences which may pose a security risk to the United States; a situation which would certainly have profound negative effects on the ability of the United States government to determine and conduct foreign policy.

NAAA has had specific interests in Mr. Bryen's case because it was an [former] NAAA employee who overheard Mr. Bryen's conversation in which he offered classified documents to representatives of a foreign government. The employee filed an affidavit with the FBI and subjected himself to a polygraph test. Subsequently, the FBI conducted an extensive investigation of this matter and collected 600 pages of material which are presently on file at the Criminal Division of the Justice Department. However, the results of this investigation into the alleged espionage violations have never been made known to us. Our Freedom of Information request concerning this investigation is 63rd on the list of projects to be undertaken by the FOI division of the Department of Justice. The Senate Armed Services Committee can obtain a copy of this file by requesting [it from the Justice Department].[5]

Similar letters were sent to members of the Senate Armed Services Committee, White House aides James A. Baker, III, and Michael Deaver, National Security Advisor Richard Allen, and Rep. Clement Zablocki, D-Wisc., Chairman of the House Foreign Affairs Committee.

Although no one confronted Perle directly in his confirmation hearings, two Senators later submitted written questions. Senator John Warner, a Virginia Republican, asked Perle to clarify the Bryen matter. Perle replied, "Dr. Stephen Bryen, a former member of the Senate Foreign Relations Committee, was investigated by the Justice Department in 1978 after it was alleged that he may have violated U.S. espionage laws. The allegations were totally unfounded, with the Justice Department dropping its investigation after concluding there was no need to carry it further. I have the highest confidence in Dr. Bryen's loyalty, patriotism and character, and I am proud he is prepared to serve his country in the Department of Defense."[6]

Senator Jeremiah Denton, of Alabama, submitted three, more detailed questions to Perle. These questions were more pointed since Joel Lisker, Denton's main staffer, had worked for John Davitt in the Justice Department and had been in charge of the Bryen case. After asking Perle whether he was aware of the investigation of Bryen, Denton stated, "My information regarding Mr. Bryen is that, while the Justice Department determined that there was insufficient evidence for indictment, *there was substantial evidence that Mr. Bryen participated in a scheme where he offered a sensitive, classified document to a representative of a foreign government.* [Emphasis added.] Further, as a result, Mr. Bryen was asked to resign his position with the Foreign Relations Committee. Please respond regarding your knowledge of the circumstances surrounding this incident."[7]

"To the best of my knowledge," Perle responded, "the allegations against Dr. Bryen were totally unfounded. Dr. Bryen's resignation from the Senate Foreign Relations Committee staff should in no way be construed as an indication of involvement in any unauthorized activity."[8]

"Do you believe," Denton asked, "it to be appropriate, given the sensitive nature of the office of International Security Policy to appoint, at any level, an individual whose reputation for integrity and loyalty to this country has been severely tarnished?"9

"I consider Dr. Bryen to be an individual of impeccable integrity," Perle said. "Of course, he is subject to the same intense security checks as is everyone serving in sensitive positions in the Department of Defense. However, I have the highest confidence in Dr. Bryen's loyalty, patriotism and character. I am pleased he is prepared to serve in the Department."10

It is rare when the Senate does not simply "rubber stamp" a Presidential nominee, particularly at the Assistant Secretary level. But Senator James Exon, a Nebraska Democrat, grew sufficiently concerned that Perle's desire to bring Bryen on board might pose a security risk. He exercised his minority party privilege and put a hold on Perle's confirmation until he had the opportunity to review the Bryen file. Exon's move set off a flurry of behind-the-scenes maneuvers to remove the final roadblock to Perle's appointment. Several Senators, presumably including Senator Henry Jackson, Perle's former boss, put pressure on Exon to lift the hold. Sources close to the scene said that the Defense Department badly needed Perle in his official capacity for an upcoming NATO conference in Europe. They promised Exon that if Perle was nominated, he could still review the Justice Department files on Bryen at a later date. Moreover, Exon was assured that Perle and Bryen would not be able to work on Middle East policies because their office was a new one, primarily responsible for East-West, European, NATO and technology transfer issues.

Exon reluctantly decided to lift the hold, apparently believing he could raise objections in the future once he reviewed the Bryen file. He explained his move this way: "My initial action in placing a hold on Mr. Perle's nomination was based on concerns I had relating to the security clearance procedures on an individual other than Mr. Perle but possibly related to the discharging of his new important responsibilities. After consultations and assurances initiated by officials in whom I have confidence with regard to security matters, I released my hold on Mr. Perle. This is all that is appropriate for me to say at this time."[11]

Exon's release on Perle came on August 3, 1981, at 11:45 A.M. The Senate then unanimously confirmed Perle's nomination and recessed for the month fifteen minutes later. Congress was on its way out of town for the summer break. Perle and Bryen, who since April had been consultants in the Pentagon as part of the Reagan transition team, moved into official Assistant Secretary and Deputy Assistant Secretary positions.

The events surrounding Perle's confirmation spread awareness about the Bryen investigation and squarely put the NAAA in the middle of the fight. I wished that Perle had been scrutinized more closely at the hearings and was disappointed that Bryen himself was never forced to answer any questions. I was heartened however, by the fact that key Senators had become concerned about the potential security risk posed by Bryen upon learning that he had been investigated for possible espionage violations.

I was also encouraged by Senator Exon's desire to obtain the Bryen file. I hoped Exon's involvement would bring us a step closer to finding out what the FBI had learned about Bryen.

The exchange between Senator Denton and Perle confirmed what had become obvious: the FBI and Justice Department had closed the Bryen investigation without bringing charges or making any kind of public announcement. The revelation forced me to face the disappointment that my encounter with Bryen in the Madison Hotel and the subsequent filing of the affidavit would not be sufficient to bring a man with Bryen's influence and connections to trial. Bryen had weathered the storm and was appointed to a critical job in the Pentagon. I felt disarmed and fearful as I pondered the prospect of a man suspected of espionage in charge of International Security Policy in the United States Pentagon.

My thoughts kept returning to the findings of the FBI investigation. Although I had to accept the fact that the case had been closed, something just did not seem right. Pletcher's statement that the case "was upsetting a few people" and Mahoney's prediction that it would go to a grand jury kept going through my mind. The fact that 600 pages on Bryen had been compiled also nagged me. Even Denton's question, which probably reflected the views of someone who worked on the case, was confusing. There was insufficient evidence to indict Bryen, but there was substantial evidence that he participated in a scheme and offered a classified document to foreign officials, Denton had said. Why was that not "substantial evidence" enough to push for an indictment? And was there additional evidence in the 600 pages that Bryen had committed other misdeeds? It seemed unbelievable that the Justice Department would compile that much data on an individual if there was no indication of unethical behavior or wrongdoing.

Every question emphasized the need for access to the file. It had been over a year and a half since the FOIA request was made. The Justice Department's excuses for not disclosing the file were getting flimsier. The fact that a U.S. Senator was not able to get it immediately upon request further increased my suspicions about the Department's intentions. After all, Bryen and those in the Justice Department were now working for the same boss: Ronald Reagan. The battle to get the file would now have to be fought against a new Administration that had every reason to keep the entire matter secret. With Bryen in a high-level position in the Defense Department, the risk he posed to national security rose dramatically. I grew more determined than ever to carry on the fight.

The NAAA also strengthened its resolve and waged a last-ditch battle to keep Bryen out of the Pentagon. Acting on Perle's statement that Bryen would be subject to intense security checks, the NAAA urged various Defense Department officials to closely scrutinize Bryen's past before granting him routine access to the nation's most sensitive military secrets. In an August 19, 1981 letter to James McCue, the DOD official responsible for security clearances, NAAA Executive Director David Sadd reminded him that NAAA previously had requested that he review the Justice Department file on Bryen.

> This information is pertinent to any security clearance for Stephen Bryen, presently a consultant in the Office of Assistant Secretary of International Security Policy.
>
> Subsequent to our previous letter, we received verbal assurance from your office that you would be properly responsive to the information. At that time, we requested written reply to our letter for our records. However, we have not as yet received this reply.
>
> Once again, we would like to request a letter from your office detailing the measures that you have taken to insure that this information regarding Bryen has been properly considered.[12]

On September 2, McCue sent Sadd a brief reply:

> This is in response to your recent letter suggesting Stephen Bryen may have violated United States espionage laws. The Department of Defense is familiar with the history of this matter. I can assure you that the record of the investigation on the case will be thoroughly reviewed before Mr. Bryen is granted access to any sensitive documents in connection with his current duties in the department.[13]

The NAAA also notified DOD General Counsel William H. Taft, IV* of the Bryen file. But in a September 28 letter Taft told the group, "The Department of Defense has reviewed the FBI investigative report regarding allegations that Mr. Bryen 'may have violated U.S. espionage laws by offering sensitive documents to Israeli government officials in the spring of 1978.' The file did not provide a sufficient basis to terminate Mr. Bryen's services [as a consultant] to the Department."[14]

The NAAA's last hope was to convince Fred C. Ikle, Undersecretary of Defense and Perle's immediate boss, that Bryen could not be trusted. However, that hope was crushed when Ikle, in an October 13 letter, informed NAAA of Bryen's new status.

> Dr. Steve Bryen is presently serving as Deputy Assistant Secretary of Defense with responsibility for East-West trade and technology matters. He has been granted the clearances necessary to perform his responsibilities.
>
> In granting the necessary security clearances, and in approving Dr. Bryen's appointment, a thorough examination was made of all pertinent files, including those to which your letter refers. It is my understanding that Assistant Secretary Richard Perle has answered all Congressional inquiries on this matter directed to him.[15]

The NAAA went through all the available channels in its attempt to block Bryen's appointment. In the final analysis, however, little was accomplished. Those who wanted Bryen in the Pentagon successfully rammed his appointment through the system. By preventing Senator Exon from seeing the file,

---

*Taft was later appointed Deputy Secretary of Defense (the number two position in the Pentagon) in early 1984.

they ensured that no outsiders became familiar with its contents. The assurances of DOD officials Taft and Ikle that the file had been reviewed were not very reassuring. They were part of the Administration that wanted to put Bryen in the Pentagon in the first place. Bryen clearly had plenty of friends in high places.

The entire episode received no attention from the major media. Except for those of us who were following Bryen's actions and paying attention to his stated policies, few people were aware of the security threat that Bryen posed, or the kinds of policies he was likely to pursue. Bryen's emphasis on militarism and his one-sided views on the Middle East threatened to become policies that would turn the entire region into a virtual bloodbath. Moreover, his apparent willingness to compromise not only his own position but the very security of the U.S. had world-wide ramifications. If Bryen the Senate staffer seemingly had been willing to offer classified documents to officials of another government, how far would he be willing to go to see that the policies he had been advocating while at JINSA actually became U.S. policy? Could the U.S. afford a policy that was so pro-Israel that even our long-time allies in the Arab world would be forced to question our integrity and sincere desire for peace? And with the Federal deficit growing at alarming rates, for how long could the U.S. economy survive the drain of tax money to Israel? If Bryen's seemingly intense hatred and distrust of the Soviet Union and Eastern Bloc countries were real and not mere rhetoric, what sort of controls would he demand on U.S. exports? And how would these controls affect our NATO allies, on whom neighborly relations with the East have a substantial impact?

It was these issues and questions which forced me to continue the search for the truth about Stephen Bryen. If I found that I had been mistaken and Bryen was innocent of compromise or wrongdoing, then at least I could trust in the good faith of our Defense officials, insofar as U.S. security was concerned. But everything I had heard, discovered and observed indicated otherwise. Bryen's policies were peace-threatening. More importantly, they seemed to put the interests of another country — Israel — ahead of U.S. national interests of integrity. What American citizen could stand for that?

CHAPTER 5

THE CASE PAPERS: A MATTER OF PRIORITIES

The events surrounding Stephen Bryen's appointment demonstrated to NAAA that it could not make a strong enough case against him without more compelling evidence of his past improprieties. Despite assertions to the contrary, such evidence probably was in the Bryen file. The Justice Department, however, was moving very slowly on the FOIA request and seemed to be hoping that NAAA would get frustrated and discontinue the entire effort. Convincing the Government to release information which it wants to withhold is a long and expensive process, and the Justice Department seemed determined to make things as difficult as possible for NAAA.

As the Justice Department continued to stall, the Reagan Administration announced it would propose changing the Freedom of Information Act so federal agencies could withhold more information from the public. A major goal of the Administration's proposal was to increase secrecy for law enforcement records held by the FBI and Justice Department. Moreover, Attorney General William French Smith announced the Reagan Administration would be more willing than its predecessor to defend in court agency decisions to withhold documents from FOIA requesters.[1]

The direction was ominous. In addition to making Bryen a

Deputy Assistant Secretary of Defense, the Reagan Administration had declared war on the Freedom of Information Act.
The NAAA's uphill battle to get the Bryen file had become
considerably steeper.

The NAAA decided to seek legal expertise. It turned to the
law firm Kirkpatrick, Lockhart, Hill, Christopher and Phillips,
which had handled one of its previous cases. The firm advised
NAAA officials to meet with Robert Belair, one of the top
Freedom of Information Act lawyers in Washington.

Belair was appalled by the Justice Department's handling of
the request. He quickly outlined the steps he would take to
expedite disclosure. Although he advised NAAA it would
probably be another couple of months before the Department
responded, he was confident that he could win release of some
of the documents in the Bryen file without going to court.
NAAA officials were satisfied that they were finally on the
right track and regretted not having come to Belair earlier.

I too was pleased that NAAA had found an FOIA expert to
take its case and felt that I needed to supplement its efforts by
doing additional research on Bryen. The Justice Department's
file would expose important facts about him in the context of
the espionage investigation, but there was more to him than
that. As the JINSA newsletter showed, Bryen had a definite
vision of what Israel needed from the United States and how it
could be obtained. I began tracking newspaper stories to learn
the extent that Bryen — and Richard Perle — were influencing
Reagan Administration policies.

An associate pointed out that Senator Clifford Case, who
had since passed away, had donated his Senate papers to the
Rutgers University Library. My associate suggested that the
papers might contain useful information about Bryen, who
had worked for Case for seven years. We called Rutgers and
discovered that the Case collection contained dozens of boxes
of documents which no one thus far had bothered to study. It

seemed a safe bet that at least some of the documents would relate to Bryen's work in the Senate. We drove to Rutgers in New Brunswick, New Jersey, to take a look at the Case papers.

We spent two full days pouring through thousands of documents. What we saw revealed that Bryen had worked to further Israeli interests from the moment Case put him in charge of foreign affairs issues in 1973. Bryen specialized in promoting more military aid to Israel, while fighting similar aid to Arab governments. He fought to ensure that he would have direct access to classified agreements between the United States and foreign nations. He also tried to downplay the importance of the Palestinian problem in the Middle East. Bryen worked long and hard, often writing 25-30 page memos to convince Senator Case and others of this viewpoint.

Clifford P. Case was elected to the House in 1944 and to the Senate in 1954. For most of his career, he was regarded as a liberal Republican from New Jersey. He championed full disclosure of Congressional members' personal finances — a stand which did not make him popular with his Senate colleagues. Case led the call for a full investigation of Bobby Baker, an aide to President Lyndon Johnson who had been accused of corruption. He also won enactment of the Case Act, which required the Executive Branch to inform Congress of secret agreements with foreign governments. By the 1970s Case had become the ranking Republican on the Senate Foreign Relations Committee.

From early in his career, Case spoke out in support of Israel. But a staffer who worked for him in the late 1960s and early 1970s said Israel was not one of his primary concerns. "He had a large Jewish constituency, so he did not want Israel to become a problem issue for him," the staffer said. "But he really was not that active when it came to Israel. He let others take the lead. That all changed when Bryen started handling foreign policy issues. He helped turn Case into a 'Republican

Henry Jackson'."[2]

A Senate staffer can greatly influence his Senator's position on issues related to his expertise. It is the staffer who does the research, briefs the Senator and writes speeches. The staffer also is responsible for legislative details. By skillfully presenting facts and problems, and lining up the necessary constituencies, an aggressive staffer can sometimes determine on what issues a Senator will focus.

Stephen Bryen first went to work for Case in 1971. It was not until 1973 that he became the person on Case's personal staff in charge of foreign policy issues. One source said Bryen and Richard Perle, then a staffer to Senator Henry Jackson, quickly became friends. "Perle took Bryen under his wing and schooled him on the ways of the Senate." They appeared to have a lot in common with their "mutual love" for Israel.[3]

Another aide to Case said Bryen and Perle were together so often they began to look like a "Mutt and Jeff" team. "They would always come charging into the office together, wanting to talk with Senator Case about some bright new idea they had. They never stopped. He had to say 'No' to them more than once," the aide said.[4]

In 1975, Case shifted Bryen from his personal staff to a spot on the Senate Foreign Relations Committee. It was a significant change because Bryen was to be Case's designated staffer on the Committee. Prior to the move, none of the Committee staffers represented any one Senator, rather, they worked for all members. Duties were divided according to issues and geography.[5]

Case's record indicates that his support for Israel intensified after Bryen took over responsibility for foreign affairs issues in 1973. Prior to that time, much of Case's pro-Israeli activities came in the form of speeches, or endorsements of resolutions and letters written by other Senators. After Bryen's arrival, Case's energies were focused on meatier issues — like arms and money.[6]

During the Israeli-Egyptian War of 1973, Senator Case was an initial co-sponsor of a resolution backing the transfer to Israel of Phantom aircraft and other equipment. Less than a month after Israel won the war, he introduced legislation to authorize $2.2 billion in emergency military assistance for Israel. A year later, he introduced a bill, later adopted by Congress but vetoed by President Ford, to cut off U.S. money for the United Nations Education, Scientific and Cultural Organization because of the anti-Israel resolutions it had adopted.[7]

In 1975, Case introduced a resolution to block the sale of HAWK surface-to-air missiles to Jordan. Although the resolution did not pass, Case was able to negotiate a compromise with the Ford Administration which restricted the mobility of the HAWK missiles and therefore eliminated them as an offensive threat.[8]

Despite opposition from the Ford Administration, in 1976 Case introduced a measure that resulted in $275 million in additional military and economic aid to Israel. Case argued that Israel needed the funding in order to buy crucial U.S. military equipment. Later that year, Case led the Senate fight against the Administration's request to sell Maverick air-to-ground missiles to Saudi Arabia. The effort led to a compromise in which the Saudis received only one third of the missiles the Administration wanted to sell.[9]

In 1977, Case opposed a new Carter Administration policy on conventional arms sales which did not include Israel in a preferred category of countries to receive advanced U.S. military equipment and military co-production. Case dropped a proposed measure to change the policy when Carter agreed to include Israel in the preferred category, and, in addition, to allow Israel to utilize U.S. military assistance to produce the Chariot tank. He also challenged a State Department proposal to sell F-15s to the Saudis, and condemned what he called the Carter Administration's "step-by-step acceptance of the PLO" and trend toward "imposition of a settlement" of the Palestinian issue.[10]

By the end of 1977, these efforts added up: Israel had become the largest recipient of aid in the annual foreign aid bill approved by Congress.[11]

Bryen surely did his best to keep Case's attentions focused on Israel's needs and the Middle East. In 1975, for instance, Bryen wrote Case a 23-page critique of the Middle East strategies espoused by George Ball, a former Assistant Secretary of State, and then Secretary of State Henry Kissinger. He began by stating that, "absent the pressure of the Superpowers, the Palestinian problem would, for the most part, be a local problem at the most and that it likely could be quietly taken care of, or would simply lose its momentum."[12]

Bryen said Ball's approach, which was shared by "Arabists" at the State Department, was based on two assumptions: (1) war in the Middle East must be avoided at all costs because it would inevitably involve the United States and the Soviets in a direct conflict; and (2) Israel must surrender all occupied territories and accept a Palestinian state of some undefined sort. Bryen disputed Ball's claim that a Palestinian state would prompt Arafat and the PLO to disavow violence. "There is no way the PLO would or could renounce further violence, since a West Bank state would be, by its very nature, nothing more than an expanded refugee camp, unprotected and unproductive," he said.[13]

A West Bank state which would return Israel to its pre-1967 borders was totally unacceptable to him. Bryen continued, "Unable to accept that reality, Israel will rather quickly go from a moderate democratic state to a right wing military-run dictatorship. In that status, Israel will attack its adversaires

[sic], it will lose American support, and, even if Israel someway manages to win the first round, its future will become a questionmark. There is no doubt that many thousands will decide to leave the country in another diaspora. The others, totally isolated, will face the Masada*.... While I think it unnecessary and avoidable this is where the Ball position gets you in the final analysis."[14]

Kissinger, whom Bryen viewed as primarily interested in furthering Rockefeller and multinational corporate interests abroad, was trying to pacify the Middle East through a huge commercial development plan financed by the United States. Although Kissinger could not be called an "Arabist," Bryen criticized his more moderate policies in the Arab world. "From Kissinger's theoretical vantage point — business and industry means moderation and a reasonable lack of hostile action," Bryen wrote. But in his view the cost would be high. "It may be that the cost of not making war in the Middle East will exceed in the long term the cost of making war in Vietnam," Bryen said. "Kissinger," he added, "has no real interest in Israel as a viable power in the Middle East since this does not serve any major purpose for the United States. While Kissinger has an emotional attachment to some kind of Jewish state this is of no real importance to the interests he serves."[15]

Bryen found more value in the approach advocated by Robert Tucker, a Johns Hopkins University professor, which surfaced in an article in Podhoretz's *Commentary* magazine. Tucker suggested that what was missing from U.S. policy in the Middle East was, in Bryen's words, "the threat of the use of force, if not the use of force itself." The Tucker approach envisages a very major change in Middle East power relationships because the United States would have to be ready to seize and hold the Saudi oil fields, he said. "It will mean, in

---

*Site of great defeat for Jews in ancient Israel.

some form, a return to a cold war scenario with the Soviets and a . . . return to a system of relationships with the rest of the world more nearly similar to the 1950's than the present day."[16]

Tucker "has a point," Bryen concluded, because the failure of Kissinger's approach will mean "the West will either have to use force to solve the energy problem or it will have to initiate a strong and workable rationing policy, or it may end up with some variant of the above [both force and rationing]."[17]

The twists and turns in Byren's arguments were not surprising. They were generally the same, although less refined, as those he later put forth in the JINSA newsletter. But since the memo was written solely for Senator Case, Bryen was less inhibited. The cold and calculating way in which Bryen rejected the need for a Palestinian state and refused to consider any ideas to help the Palestinian people was predictable. To him, the Palestinians merely posed "a local problem" for Israel. They were not capable, according to Bryen, of operating a government — only an expanded refugee camp. The memo certainly seemed to me to have racist undertones.

Bryen's view of the Palestinians was rooted in the need to justify the displacement and continuing oppression of them by the Israelis. Throughout history, the controlling classes — whether they were Romans, Spanish conquistadors, U.S. slaveowners or Nazis — always created a racist philosophy to explain the need for genocide and ruthless exploitation. In his efforts to bolster U.S. support for Israeli dominance over the Palestinians, Bryen participated in an age-old tradition.

While Bryen showed no sympathy towards Palestinians, he often tried to garner pity for Israel. In a March 18, 1977 memo to Case, Bryen claimed the Carter Administration was putting undue pressure on Israel in order to enhance relations with moderate Arab states. The United States placed what Bryen viewed as "severe restraints" on Israel after its excursion into southern Lebanon, and allowed the Saudis to help manage the conflict. Carter also had endorsed a Palestinian homeland, Bryen said, signaling a tilt toward the PLO. "The probability is this is the first 'tilt' among many 'tilts' that will be coming. U.S. policy is driven by the evident weakness of the cornerstones of its Arab policies — the political flabbiness of Sadat and the probability that he is double dealing more and more with the Soviets; the possibilities of a transition in Saudi Arabia which could stir up a real hornets nest for U.S. foreign policy in the area. The stakes are going up increasingly and the obvious scapegoat is not hard to find. Under the circumstances some consideration had to be given on how to protect the scapegoat from its potential political fate," Bryen said.[18]

Six months later, following high level Middle East talks between the United States and the Soviet Union, Bryen wrote another memo entitled "Pressure and Threats Against Israel." "Over the last two weeks the administration launched an all out pressure campaign against Israel with three objectives," he wrote. According to the memo, the first was to get Israel to withdraw from southern Lebanon; the second to halt Israeli settlements on the West Bank; and the third to convince Israel to accept a Palestinian representative at the proposed peace conference in Geneva. "The U.S. has been negotiating for three weeks with the Soviets on how to bring the PLO into the Geneva conference and how to get Israel to agree to an eventual Palestinian state," Bryen continued. "The joint statement reached with the Soviets, as a consequence, contained all the rhetoric of Soviet Arab demands, threatened not only Israel but the political viability of Egypt and Jordan, and was another setback for a negotiated settlement. Israel was not informed beforehand of this Soviet draft declaration which the U.S. accepted with modest changes . . . . The U.S. is prepared, to offer with guarantees, the creation of a Palestinian state on the West Bank of the Jordan. For this Israel will get some kind of assurances from the Soviets and the U.S. or from the U.N. —none of which are substitutes for Israel's security needs. It is to be wondered the way this operation has been put together whether the U.S. can be seen any longer as a reliable partner in the search for peace."[19]

In January 1978, Bryen, who had become staff director for the Foreign Relations Subcommittee on Near Eastern and South Asian Affairs, wrote a 30-page memo on the Middle East negotiations for Subcommittee members. Bryen said the "Arab propaganda attack has focused" on the Israeli settlements because eliminating them would mean "throwing back the 'Zionist enemy'." The settlement also represented the most important issue for Israel, he said. Bryen continued:

> Israel is a country that has relied historically on settlements as part of its nation-building process. The settlements are outposts of security, they are also very important in motivating the "citizen army" to behave tenaciously in combat. More significantly the settlements are an immense important window on Israel's enemies. The presence of Jews in alien places is a critical barometer in estimating intentions and halting political erosion.

> While it is very hard to tie up the Israeli view of its security in any neat knot, perhaps it can be summarized this way, 'If we get kicked out of the territories, then whatever you call it you have a Palestinian state. If you have a Palestinian state, then there is no reason to suppose that Jordan will not crumble from within. A dangerous leadership will emerge, tied together with this new state and with Syria politically. It will be radical.'

It goes without saying, considering the above, that the security arrangements arrived at for the area are as much at the heart of the problem as is the question of Palestinian "self rule" or "self-determination", or more important than whether you call the PLO terrorists or freedom fighters.[20]

In February, Bryen wrote Case a three-page memo which reflected his sense of urgency. Entitled "The Coming War in the Middle East," the memo expressed the view that the Syrians thought they could win a limited victory over Israel and were willing to fight alone. "The war," wrote Bryen, "will be started as soon as Syria is certain that she can pacify Lebanon sufficiently to withdraw her forces from there." Bryen also asserted that the Russians would be likely to provide air cover. "This means that despite American efforts, which have become recently desperate to try and get Israel to concede almost everything ahead of time, the Soviets foresee they have a free field of activity ahead for themselves. Their main hope is that the United States will not have the will to assist Israel until it is too late, if the Soviets come into a kind of direct clash with Israel."[21]

Between 1975 and 1978, Bryen consistently argued for Congressional pressure which would help Israel maintain its grip on the West Bank and deflect Carter Administration hopes to negotiate the creation of a Palestinian homeland. Emerging from Bryen's memos was the urgent theme that Israel's very existence was at stake. Bryen portrayed any effort by the Carter Administration to negotiate an even-handed, peaceful settlement in the region as a "tilt" toward the Palestinians, a tilt that he claimed would bring death to Israel. Israel's enemies were depicted as ready and anxious to attack — with full support of the Soviets — if the United States lowered its guard, and Bryen did not hesitate to use exaggeration and alarmist pronunciations to keep Case and other pro-Israel Senators sufficiently concerned.

Bryen also worked closely with Senator Richard Stone, a Florida Democrat, who was chairman of the Foreign Relations Subcommittee on Near Eastern Affairs. In the months preceding Bryen's Madison Hotel meeting with the Israelis, there was growing concern over the sale of jets to Saudi Arabia, the nation that Israel perceived as the greatest threat to its relationship with the United States. On February 27, 1978, ten days before the Madison Hotel incident, Stone issued a six-page statement on the dangers posed by the Saudi's new air base at Tabuk. Stone wrote:

> According to reports from Foreign Relations Com-mittee staff members, this air base at Tabuk, Saudi Arabia is becoming more offensive in nature than defensive. It is less than 100 miles from Elat, Israel's chief port. Yet it is more than 800 miles from Saudi Arabia's closest oil fields.
>
> When HAWK missiles were supplied to Saudi Arabia, the Pentagon told us they were to be used defensively to protect valuable oil fields. Now we have learned from good sources that, in fact HAWK missiles are positioned at Tabuk right next to Israel.
>
> It has long been U.S. policy not to sell weapons to states that might use them to threaten Israel. But the HAWKS poised in Tabuk may cover Israeli airspace. Have our military experts advised the President of this? What are the facts about this Saudi military installation? What has Congress been told? What has the President been told? Does this situation at Tabuk increase the offensive risk of selling F-15 aircraft to Saudi Arabia?[22]

Stone's speech, which sounded like it may have been

written by Bryen, indicated that the Saudi's Tabuk air base had caught the Israeli military off guard. It also suggested that Israeli intelligence agents had informed Foreign Relations Committee staff members of their surprise. Stone was particularly interested in seeing what information the Pentagon had on the bases, and seemed to view the base at Tabuk only in terms of Israeli military strategy. He did not stop to mention Saudi Arabia's interests in having a base at Tabuk, such as protection of the holy cities of Mecca and Medina.

My mind flashed back to the Madison Hotel meeting and Bryen's comments about another document. Bryen had said, "I have the Pentagon document on the bases, which you are welcome to see." After reading the Stone speech, and analyzing it in the context of current events, I saw more clearly why the document would have been so important to the Israelis, and how Bryen would have been in the perfect position to get it. After all, the chairman of the subcommittee for which he worked had just made a major speech inquiring about the Pentagon's knowledge of the bases.

As we finished looking through the Case papers, I realized that we had seen no references to the Bryen investigation. I thumbed through the pile one more time and found a one page memo, stuck between some xeroxed newspaper clippings, that almost made me fall off my chair. The names were crossed out, but by holding the memo up to the light it was easy to read the familiar "To: Senator Case, From: Steve Bryen." The memo said the Carter Administration lacked the votes in Congress to win approval of the "package deal" sales to Saudi Arabia, Egypt and Israel. It read:

Therefore, the administration will offer a "compromise," if they can get takers. The substance of the compromise will be _more_ airplanes for Israel!

The now "famous" meeting I had at the Madison with Israel's top man in the Defense Ministry had as its basic conclusion the following pertinent information regarding Israel's aircraft purchase.

(1) Israel cannot afford to pay for more airplanes.

(2) Israel cannot afford to buy the 75 F-16s offered to her in the "package."

(3) It is unlikely that Israel will be able to purchase any more than 50 F-16s by 1980-1981.

(4) The administration is aware fully that Israel cannot afford the additional airplanes and does not plan to offer more military assistance to make it possible for her to purchase more. The administration also cut off the possibility of coproduction of the F-16, which would have lowered per unit costs and made it financially possible for Israel to buy more planes.

(5) The Budget Committee will not authorize any more security supporting assistance funds this year so the chance to increase funds for Israel to enable her to buy more aircraft is out of the question.

This is the essence of the problem created by the arms sale and the search for a compromise. The sixty planes for Saudi Arabia is just too much to deal with, more than two times too much under the circumstances. In consideration of any "compromise" these are the key salient facts to have in mind.[23]*

I left the Rutgers library thinking about Bryen's account of the Madison meeting. He said the bottom line was Israel's lack of money. Only with massive increases in U.S. aid could Israel

---

*See Appendix B for Bryen memo

get the jets it wanted.

When I got back to Washington, I pulled my affidavit out of the file to see how it squared with Bryen's memo. The affidavit quoted Bryen as saying, "We can make them bargain," when the Israelis expressed concern about getting the arms they needed from the United States. It seemed likely that Bryen thought they could bargain for more U.S. aid as part of the package deal. He also told the Israelis, "I hope you have good R&D and get ready to convert it into weapons.

It's not a bad airplane I've flown in it myself. Can you make it yourself?" The Israeli replied, "Yes, we don't have to buy it."

It all fit rather nicely. Bryen and the Israelis believed they could still get the aircraft at a lower price by setting up a coproduction agreement with the United States. But as the Bryen memo noted, the Carter Administration nixed the strategy.

Bryen's candid assessment of Israel's cash-flow problems made me think about the Camp David Accords, which were signed six months after the Madison incident. Much of the media focused on the return of the Sinai to Egypt, and the vague agreement to consider a Palestinian homeland, which never came to pass. For Israel, the main benefit of the Accords was the billions of dollars in U.S. military aid. Aid to Israel was nearly doubled, and the increase probably enabled Israel to buy the jets that were offered in the package deal. So while Israel did not get more aid as part of the package deal, it was able to strike an even better bargain at Camp David. Begin realized how badly Carter wanted a peace agreement, so he put a price tag of over 5 billion dollars on Israel's participation. The money undoubtedly came in the nick of time and helped Israel avert attention from its economic difficulties, which were exacerbated by the arms build up. The Israelis were very sensitive about their ailing economy. It was a core weakness which did not fit in with the image they wanted to portray to the world. Yet on that fateful day in the Madison Hotel, Israeli defense officials bluntly told their trusted ally that they needed lots of money — fast. Bryen, in turn, was one of the first to carry the message to pro-Israeli politicians. Six months later, America got the Camp David Accords and Israel got an economic bail out. It was an aid increase of unprecedented proportions, but it did not solve Israel's long-term economic problems. They would return to haunt America in the years to come.

During the summer and fall of 1982, as I stepped up my research of Bryen and the NAAA retained Belair for the FOIA battle, another series of events took place which affected me greatly: the Israeli invasion of Lebanon and the encirclement and shelling of Beirut. The Israelis had made excursions into southern Lebanon before, but had never launched an invasion of this scale for the avowed purposes of forcing the PLO out of Lebanon. As Bryen noted in one of his memos to Case, earlier Israeli actions in southern Lebanon had drawn stiff opposition and pressure from the Carter Administration. The Reagan Administration, however, seemed to turn the other cheek until the daily Israeli shelling of Beirut and the horrific massacres at the Sabra and Shatilla refugee camps dominated U.S. network newscasts and spurred public cries for a solution.

The evacuation of the PLO did not come until all sides agreed to a settlement whereby a multi-national peacekeeping force, consisting of United States, French, Italian and British troops, would be stationed in Lebanon. The idea found widespread support both in the United States and abroad, as everyone was anxious to spare Beirut from total annihilation. Although I was pleased that the effort temporarily halted the gunfire and forced the Israelis to move out of the city, it still made me feel uneasy to think of American troops stationed in a hot spot like Beirut, where there are so many groups willing to fight and kill. It seemed likely that the cease-fire would not last forever, and that the U.S. troops, at least, would get caught in the crossfire. If that happened, what would be Reagan's response? He was not the kind of President who would shy away from battle. But the alternative of staying seemed like a no-win situation.

I thought about the new developments in the context of Stephen Bryen's writings. In the JINSA newsletter, and in some of his memos as a Senate staffer, Bryen consistently pushed for a United States military presence in the Middle East. He clearly thought the U.S. presence would benefit Israel. Now it appeared that Bryen's dream strategy for the Middle East was coming true. The U.S. Marines were there — just a few miles from the shores of Tripoli [Lebanon]. Yet for the Marines, and for the United States, Bryen's dream would quickly become a nightmare. Meanwhile, Israel would emerge as the main beneficiary.

CHAPTER 6

THE INVESTIGATION OF STEPHEN BRYEN

The in-depth look at Stephen Bryen's writings for Senator Clifford Case and for the JINSA newsletter removed any doubts that he was a pro-Israeli crusader who devoted a good deal of his time to "the cause." Although his writings did not suggest that Bryen had done anything illegal, they certainly raised questions of to whom he was most loyal: the United States, or Israel? Given such important questions of loyalty, one must question the prudence of putting Bryen in a U.S. Government position — either in the Senate or the Pentagon — in which he would enjoy regular access to our nation's most sensitive military serets. Many more questions arose about Bryen's loyalties and actions, and each one of them emphasized the need to get the Justice Department's file on the investigation. If I could learn so much about Bryen through publicly available sources of information, then assuredly the Justice Department and FBI agents, with their vast resources, skills and experience, must have been able to gather much more information about his actions.

I soon learned that federal investigators had uncovered a lot of damaging information on Bryen. By December 1982, Bob Belair had gotten results: the Justice Department had disclosed a portion of the Bryen file to the NAAA. The most startling document among those released was a January 26, 1979, "Action Memorandum," written by John H. Davitt, Chief of the Department's Internal Security Section, to Assistant Attorney General Philip B. Heymann, head of the Criminal Division. Davitt, who headed the team in charge of the day-to-day investigation of Bryen, clearly advocated a grand jury probe of Bryen.

> The first option is to discontinue further investigation as it now stands thus leaving many unanswered questions.... The second option and the one which we urge strongly is to complete this important inquiry before an investigative grand jury. Some of the unresolved questions thus far, which suggest that Bryen is (a) gathering classified information for the Israelis, (b) acting as their unregistered agent and (c) lying about it, are as follows:[1]*

The next five-and-one-half pages, which must have summarized extensive evidence against Bryen, were completely blacked out. The Justice Department asserted the information could be withheld under various FOIA exemptions. This was an odd claim. The document disclosed the investigators' conclusions and recommendations — possibly the most damaging aspect to Bryen. Yet the Department withheld the facts underlying those conclusions and recommendations. Why were the facts covered up while the recommendation for a grand jury was released?

Another memo further increased our suspicions. It was dated April 26, 1978 — eight months prior to the Davitt recommendation of grand jury action — and sent by Benjamin Civiletti, Heymann's predecessor in the Criminal Division, to the Director of the Federal Bureau of Investigation.

---

* See Appendix C for "Action Memorandum" of John Davitt, Chief, Internal Security Section, Criminal Division to Philip B. Heymann, Assistant Attorney General, Criminal Division, January 26, 1979.

On April 18, 1978, an attorney of this Division received information from a Congressional staff aide that an individual identified to him as Stephen Bryen, who allegedly has been temporarily suspended from his position on the Hill in the face of a Department of Justice investigation concerning him, may have been disclosing classified information to the Government of Israel over a period of years. The source of the information said that if the following individuals were interviewed that "he was 98 percent sure" that they would verify the allegations against Bryen.

The three potential witnesses are former associates of Bryen: [names blacked out under FOIA privacy exemptions]. According to the source, each of these witnesses will verify that Bryen has, in the past, discussed his activities with them.[2]*

The "Action Memorandum" and the Civiletti memo were two of several documents in the 100 pages disclosed by the Justice Department. The Department withheld an additional 50 pages under FOIA exemptions protecting pre-decisional recommendations of government attorneys, confidential sources, privacy and national security. Attached to the disclosures was a December 28, 1982, cover letter from Douglas Wood, head of the Criminal Division's FOIA/Privacy Act Unit, which stated the unthinkable:

This is in response to your request of April 25, 1980, for access to records concerning Stephen D. Bryen.

A search of the Criminal Division's central index revealed that there were records within the scope of

---

* See Appendix D for memorandum of Benjamin R. Civiletti, Assistant Attorney General, Criminal Division, to Director, Federal Bureau of Investigation, April 26, 1979.

your request in the Internal Security Section. *After an exhaustive search, however, these records could not be located.* Fortunately the attorney responsible for this matter kept a "working file" which should contain most of the records contained in the original. There is no way, however, to identify what records, if any, were missing. [Emphasis added.][3]*

In its initial response in 1980, the Justice Department had advised NAAA that there were 600 pages responsive to its FOIA request. The fact that the Department said it could locate only 150 of these meant there was a whopping 450-page gap. To where did the 450 pages mysteriously vanish?

Revelations that federal investigators considered the possibility that Bryen was an Israeli spy, coupled with the inexplicable disappearance of most of the file, hardened the NAAA's resolve to pursue its rights under the Freedom of Information Act. On April 6, 1983, the NAAA filed an FOIA lawsuit in a federal court in Washington to require the Department to find the missing documents and hand over those which the law required be made public. In a letter to the Justice Department, Bob Belair assailed the Department's poor performance:

In view of the nature and history of this matter, it hardly needs stating that NAAA finds the Department's response of December 28th to be unacceptable. From a legal standpoint, the response indicates a shocking disregard on the Department's part for the rights of NAAA, or, for that matter, any FOIA

---

* See Appendix E for letter of Douglas S. Wood, Chief, Freedom of Information/Privacy Act Unit, Criminal Division, to J.R. Abinader, National Association of Arab-Americans, December 28, 1982.

requestor, and for the Department's responsibilities under the FOIA.

From a policy standpoint, the Department's response is even more upsetting. NAAA's FOIA request seeks information about a government investigation which lasted over a year, and which investigated charges that an individual who is now a high Pentagon official violated United States espionage laws by providing classified information to officials of the Israeli Government. Given the importance of this matter to American security interests, it is inconceivable that the Department of Justice could identify responsive documents, state that the documents total 600 pages, acknowledge that the documents are subject to an outstanding FOIA request, and then, just at the point after two and one-half years when the request comes up for processing, lose all 600 pages of the documents. We find this to be a bitterly disappointing and frankly ominous development.[4]

The filing of the NAAA lawsuit prompted the Justice Department to action. Within a few weeks, word leaked out that it had located the Bryen file. We learned that it had been in the office of White House Counsel Fred Fielding. Not only did the government find the missing 600 pages, it sheepishly admitted that the FBI had in its possession an additional 400 pages on the Bryen probe. Moreover, it disclosed for the first time that some documents in the Bryen file originated from the Department of Defense, the National Security Agency and the Central Intelligence Agency.

The "discovery" of the file in April 1983 set off a legal tug-of-war between the Justice Department and NAAA which is still continuing. The judge for the NAAA's lawsuit was Thomas A. Flannery, a no-nonsense jurist who decades earlier had been the U.S. Attorney handling the corruption case against Bobby Baker, an aide to President Lyndon Johnson. The Justice Department clearly understood that Judge Flannery would not tolerate any more stonewalling or foot-dragging. Accordingly, it moved quickly to dig through the hundreds of pages of the Bryen file to find material it could disclose to NAAA.

Many of the hundreds of pages released by the Justice Department to the NAAA, however, were rendered incomprehensible by heavy deletions which the Department claimed were justified by FOIA exemptions. In some cases, entire pages were blacked out. In other cases, the Department withheld entire documents, claiming that they were so filled with exempt data that not a fraction of them could be released. These included a five-page "discrepancy chart", transcripts of investigators' interviews with Bryen's colleagues on the Senate Foreign Relations Committee staff and Congressional documents examined by investigators. The Department was adamant about shielding the five-and-one-half pages of the Davitt "Action Memorandum" that were blacked out. Why would the Department release Davitt's recommendation but not the supporting facts? Belair fought back. He argued that the Justice Department was badly misinterpreting the FOIA's requirements, and urged Judge Flannery to order disclosure of much of the withheld material — particularly the entire Davitt memo. The case is pending as of this writing.

The Justice Department's obstinance was frustrating to those of us who wanted to critically examine the Bryen investigation. It denied us important details and prolonged the litigation. Nonetheless, the documents disclosed by the Department provided enough information to reveal why its investigation of Bryen rapidly progressed beyond his conversation in the Madison Hotel in March of 1978. The documents suggested that once federal agents began focusing on Bryen, they discovered he consistently took part in a series of suspicious actions and maintained relationships that served Israeli interests. My suspicions that Bryen may have been offering the Israelis classified information seemed to be well-founded.

The Bryen file also confirmed that this was not an ordinary criminal investigation. As Davitt had indicated to me during our interview in 1978, the investigation centered primarily on whether Bryen had violated espionage laws by handing over secret data to the Israelis or breached the Foreign Agents Registration Act by holding a U.S. Government position and acting on behalf of a foreign power. Seldom in American history have U.S. officials been investigated for suspected violations of either law.

The investigation involved an unusual cast of characters. Many Senate Foreign Relations Committee staff members were interviewed by the FBI. The Committee's counsel became involved when Justice Department investigators wanted access to documents held by the Committee.

On the government's side, the initial investigator was FBI agent Stephen Pletcher of the Bureau's Washington Field Office. Only a few months after the investigation began, however, Pletcher left the Bureau and was replaced by FBI agent Tim Mahoney. It was never made clear why Pletcher suddenly left the FBI, but sources suggest that one reason was his dissatisfaction over the handling of the Bryen probe.[5]

Conducting the Jusice Department investigation was Joel Lisker, head of the Criminal Division's Foreign Agents Registration Unit of the Department of Justice. Lisker reported to John Davitt, chief of the Internal Security Section.*

---

*In 1981, Joel Lisker became staff director of the Senate Judiciary Subcommittee on Terrorism and John Davitt retired.

Davitt's superior was Robert Keuch, Deputy Assistant Attorney General of the Criminal Division. Benjamin Civiletti, the Assistant Attorney General who headed the Criminal Division, became Attorney General shortly after the investigation had begun. He was replaced by Philip B. Heymann, a Harvard Law Professor and veteran of the Justice and State Departments. Heymann was aided by Special Assistant Ronald Stern, also of Harvard Law School.

Another key participant was Bryen's lawyer, Nathan Lewin. Lewin was a member of Miller, Cassidy, Larocca & Lewin, the Washington law firm which represented President Nixon after the Watergate scandal forced his resignation. Lewin was an active supporter of Israel and Jewish causes, and took part in many pro-Israel organizations and demonstrations. His impressive resume listed experience as a Harvard Law professor, U.S. Supreme Court clerk and official of the Justice and State Departments.[6] He was also a friend of Phil Heymann, who made many of the key decisions in the investigation. While some Department officials knew this, they said that they did "not appreciate the depth of their friendship."[7]

I remembered from the early days of the probe how FBI agent Pletcher had impressed me as an aggressive investigator who was determined to ferret out the truth. But it was only when I began reviewing the Bryen file that I realized how aggressive Pletcher actually was. Pletcher first interviewed Bryen on April 25, 1978. He pressed Bryen to submit to a polygraph, and Bryen said he would have to talk it over with the Senators on the Foreign Relations Committee.[8] The next day, the Department of Justice opened a formal criminal investigation of Bryen.[9] Pletcher immediately set out to talk to Bryen's colleagues on the Committee staff and to dig into Bryen's past.

By May 8, 1978, when Pletcher interviewed Bryen for the second time, Pletcher already seemed suspicious of Bryen's actions. He advised Bryen that the investigation had gone "much further" than my initial report. He told him that the FBI had "a good circumstantial case against" Zvi Rafiah, a counselor at the Israeli Embassy with whom Bryen had a close relationship. Pletcher implied that Rafiah had given Bryen "orders" which Bryen had carried out. Pletcher also charged that Rafiah was behind Congressional efforts to disapprove the sale of I-Hawk missiles to Jordan, an effort in which Bryen was very active, and that Bryen was responsible for casting a cloud over the Foreign Relations Committee. In response, Bryen flatly denied that his activities in the Congressional battle over the I-Hawk missiles were attributable to requests or orders from Rafiah or from the Embassy of Israel.[10]

Bryen told Pletcher that he did not remember all the details of his conversation with the Israelis in the Madison, and said he had to rely on my affidavit to reconstruct the sequence of the conversation. Bryen asked Pletcher if the FBI sought to question the Israelis with whom he met. Pletcher replied this had not been done because such information would be "tainted," and that FBI agents "would never be given permission" to ask the Israelis for their account of the conversation.[11]

Pletcher repeatedly pressed Bryen to submit to a polygraph exam, but Bryen claimed he was advised not to do so by Senators Case, Sparkman and Stone. Pletcher responded by warning Bryen that the FBI report "probably would be leaked," and that the report would be very damaging to Bryen personally, to the Foreign Relations Committee, to Israel and the United States.[12]

After this warning from Pletcher, Bryen spoke with his new attorney, Nathan Lewin. Lewin quickly sent off a letter to John Davitt, assailing Pletcher's tactics and accusing the Justice Department of letting itself be used as a "means of keeping an honorable and law-abiding public servant from highly important duties during a particularly critical period."[13]

The documents released by the Justice Department did not disclose the specific evidence which had stirred Pletcher's suspicions, but they did provide some important clues. First was Bryen's involvement in the Jordanian I-Hawk missile affair. In 1977, Bryen accompanied Senator Stone on a fact-finding trip to the Middle East. Their first stop was Jordan. Stone then departed for Tunisia, while Bryen decided to remain in Amman, Jordan for the afternoon before heading for Israel the next day. After Stone left, Bryen asked Tom Pickering, the U.S. Ambassador to Jordan, for documents concerning the I-Hawk missile locations in Jordan. Without putting anything in writing, Bryen asked Pickering for the latest data on the Jordanian missiles, including map locations and an indication of their range. Pickering provided a briefing, but mentioned that he did not have the latest data on the missile sites due to recent changes. This information was "highly important since the objective was to keep the Hawks non-mobile and out of Israel's airspace."[14]

The Defense Department also rejected this request on grounds that Bryen did not have a need to know the information. The DOD said the material was top secret, was considered highly sensitive to Jordan's defense posture and would risk the United States' credibility if it was used improperly. The Pentagon also charged that Bryen's request did not conform to normal procedures for the transfer of classified documents to the Hill, and offered to provide Senator Stone with a briefing.[15] Bryen apparently never followed up on this offer.[16]

The Justice Department directed the FBI to find out whether Bryen had initiated the Senate Foreign Relations Committee's interest in the I-Hawk data. On June 20, FBI agents interviewed Bryen a third time. Without mentioning the I-Hawks, they asked him what procedures were normally followed by Committee staffers to obtain classified data.[17]

Bryen replied that a written request is made.[18]* Considering that Bryen tried to get the data through an oral request, and then gave up when the request was rejected, Bryen's answer undoubtedly struck investigators as a discrepancy. Later, FBI agents were allowed to review the Committee's I-Hawk-related documents without prior review by Bryen, Lewin or the Senators.[19]** However, the Bryen file did not reveal what conclusions investigators reached.

Investigators also noticed that in the weeks preceeding the Madison Hotel conversation, Senator Stone sent a letter to the Pentagon requesting top-secret photographs of the Saudi air base at Tabuk. The letter stated that if Defense officials had any questions, they should get in touch with Stephen Bryen.[20] About two weeks after the Madison incident, the Defense Department denied Stone access to the documents.[21] Investigators were beginning to see a pattern develop in which Bryen invoked Senator Stone's name in unsuccessful efforts to get classified U.S. military secrets that would have been of great interest to the Israeli defense establishment.

A primary focus of the investigation was the so-called "document on the bases," which I overheard Bryen offer to the Israeli defense team in the Madison. On March 8, 1978, one day before the Madison meeting, the Senate Foreign Relations Committee received a document from the Pentagon entitled, "DOD Analysis of Saudi Request To Purchase F-15 Fighter Aircraft." The document was stamped "Secret — NoForn," meaning that it was classified and was not to be

---

*See Appendix F for Memorandum of Ronald A. Stern, Special Assistant to the AAG, Criminal Division, to Philip B. Heymann, October 12, 1978.

**See Appendix G for Memorandum of Joel S. Lisker, Chief, Registration Unit, Internal Security Section, to John H. Davitt, Chief, Internal Security Section, Criminal Division, September 26, 1979.

given to foreigners. The fact that the Committee received this document the night before Bryen met with the Israelis must have seemed like more than a coincidence to the increasingly skeptical investigators. In earlier interviews, Bryen denied possessing a document on the bases, discussing a document on the bases or offering the Israelis a document on the bases. Bryen later admitted to investigators that he might have discussed a document on the Saudi base at Tabuk, but claimed that it would have been an unclassified summary of the classified Tabuk document.[22]

Investigators concentrated on the F-15 document. They asked the Defense Intelligence Agency to determine whether it could be considered a "document on the bases," and whether it would have been of high value to the Israelis. They also checked the document for fingerprints of Bryen and Zvi Rafiah. The Justice Department's file indicated that Bryen's fingerprints were found all over the F-15 document,[23] but did not divulge whether Rafiah's prints were found.*

After reviewing reports of the three FBI interviews with Bryen, Joel Lisker, head of the Justice Department's Foreign Agent Registration Unit and the primary official in charge of the probe, drew up a large "discrepancy chart" and a three-page analysis to go with it.[24] The Justice Department also directed FBI agents to go through the Senate Foreign Relations Committee files for material on the I-Hawk matter.

In September 1978, Nathan Lewin learned of the investigators' plans to examine Committee files, and also discovered that there were discrepancies in Bryen's stories. On September 25, Lewin wrote the first of a series of letters directly to Philip Heymann, the Assistant Attorney General in charge of the Criminal Division, to protest what he called the "extended duration" of the investigation and the "totally unjustified"

---

* See Appendix F.

request for the Committee documents on the I-Hawks. Lewin told Heymann that Bryen was merely doing his job in checking the latest status of the Jordanian missiles and that any allegations of impropriety were "outrageous." Lewin added, "The record of this investigation demonstrates that it has been conducted sloppily and unfairly."[25]

Lewin's complaint must have convinced Heymann that he needed to assign his Special Assistant, Ron Stern, to keep tabs on the case. The second week in October, 1978, Stern gave Heymann a progress report in a lengthy memo.

> The investigation is virtually complete. A report on the Committee documents reviewed by the FBI on 10/10 must be received and analyzed and there is one other interview to be conducted. While Lisker remains suspicious of Bryen, the investigation has not disclosed a basis for criminal prosecution.[26]*

Stern downplayed the importance of vital evidence in explaining his conclusion to Heymann.

> The FBI has found 9 latent prints of Bryen's on a classified DOD report on the Saudi Arabian request to purchase F-15s from the United States. This report was supplied to the Senate Foreign Relations Committee on 3/8/78 — the day before the 3/9 meeting. That report, however, does not concern bases. Senator Stone had requested a report on a Saudi base at Tabuk by letter of 2/23/78 but this request was refused by DOD on 3/24/78. It is not clear what report on bases Bryen could have had on 3/9, unless he found another means to secure the information on Tabuk.

> "The Pentagon document" question is appropriately the key concern of Internal Security. There is no

---

*See Appendix F.

evidence that Bryen passed such a document or offered one to the Israelis other than Saba's affidavit. Bryen's fingerprints on the F-15 document are not very probative since Bryen would have reviewed this document as part of his staff function and since the document is not about "bases."27*

About a month later, the FBI and Lisker were provided with an expert opinion which directly challenged Stern's conclusion that the F-15 report was not a "document on the bases." Responding to the Justice Department's earlier request for an analysis of the F-15 report, a key Defense Intelligence Agency [DIA] analysis concluded that the report could in fact be considered a "document on the bases," and that it would be of tremendous value to Israeli defense officials. In a November 20, 1978 letter to FBI agent Timothy Mahoney [who by then had replaced Pletcher], DIA officer Edward M. Collins explained the DIA's interpretation:

> The enclosure to this memorandum addresses two questions concerning the unauthorized disclosure of the subject document. The answer to the question of whether the document could be described as "a document on the bases" requires some interpretation. In a strict intelligence sense, the document cannot be described as such. It is entirely conceivable, however, that a person not directly involved with intelligence would describe it as "a document on bases." *Therefore, our position, with reservations as outlined in the enclosure, is that the document is "a document on the bases."* [Emphasis added.]

> The second question addressed the intelligence value of the document and the effect of the release of its information. *Our review of the document leads to the*

---

*See Appendix F.

conclusion that it would be of high intelligence value to the suspected recipient nation. [Emphasis added.] Disclosure could adversely affect US relations with several Middle Eastern nations, US intelligence collection activities, future US arms sales negotiations, the course of battle in future Middle Eastern wars, and authorized US intelligence exchanges with foreign governments. Full details of the intelligence value of the document and possible ramifications of its disclosure are given in the enclosure to the memorandum.[28]*

The enclosed analysis revealed that the DOD document Bryen had in hand on the eve of his Madison meeting was an extremely valuable document, classified top secret, and labeled "WARNING NOTICE — SENSITIVE INTELLIGENCE SOURCES AND METHODS INVOLVED —NOT RELEASABLE TO FOREIGN NATIONALS."

Much of the DIA's analysis of the document was blacked out under FOIA exemptions. Those portions left intact read as follows:

1. The document as a description of military bases.

(U) This document cannot be considered as one on military bases by any strict definition. This is because it does not contain specific descriptions, such as unit deployments, physical facilities, static defenses, access routes, precise geographical locations, etc. for any bases. The document could be considered as addressing military bases under a more liberal definition, however, since the general locations, functions, and antiaircraft defenses for all major Saudi military bases are con-

---

*See Appendix H for letter of DIA officer Edward M. Collins to Timothy D. Mahoney, Federal Bureau of Investigation, November 20, 1978.

tained in this document. It must be pointed out that the main subject of this document is Saudi Arabian military capabilities and defense requirements — not Saudi Arabian military bases . . . .

2.b. Information on Saudi Arabia [Five lines deleted] document contains an extensive description of Saudi air force and air defense capabilities, doctrine and plans [two more paragraphs deleted]. This section also contains the rationale behind the air force's current fighter deployments, and proposed deployments after craft. [Eight lines deleted] . . .

3. The release of Section III (Current Saudi Arabian Air Defense Systems) is probably the most damaging aspect of this incident. This section reveals the entire Saudi Arabia air defense organization. Systems discussed include radar networks, sector-operation centers, the air defense command center, anti-aircraft artillery assets, HAWK and Redeye surface-to-air missiles (SAMs) and Lightning and F-5 Fighter aircraft [Ten lines deleted] . . . .

6. The portions of Section VI (Appropriateness of the Saudi Request for 60 F-15s) which would be of high value to Israel are the portions on absorption ability and aircraft configurations. [Ten lines deleted] . . . .

c. Information on Iran.

c.1. Information concerning Iranian armed forces would be extremely valuable to Israel. [Nine lines deleted]. The information on Iranian air force, particularly the inventory and "negative capability" statements (where Iranian capabilities are less than would normally be expected), would be of singular value to the Israelis. Israeli relations with Iran have not been antagonistic over the years, as they have been with Arab countries. [Two paragraphs deleted]. In short, the US ability to accurately assess Iranian capabilities may be degraded by this compromise . . . .

d. Information on Israel.

1. The disclosure of the information concerning the Israeli armed forces presents an unique problem in that we are faced with Israelis having obtained our candid assessment of their own military establishment. [Eight lines deleted]. Disclosure of the information on page 11-15 could prove to be a major embarrassment to the US Government. [Two lines deleted]. Placed in the wrong hands, such information would not serve the best interest of the U.S. Government . . . .

3. Appendix A is particularly damaging to the US Government [Five lines deleted].[29]*

The memo also said that the DOD document's information on the armed forces of Kuwait and Sudan would be of high value to Israel. As for data on the People's Democratic Republic of Yemen [PDRY], the DIA said, "This information would be of extremely high value to Israel due to the potential threat the PDRY poses to Israeli shipping through the Straits of Bab al Mandeb."[30]**

The Defense Intelligence Agency analysis put the entire Bryen matter in a whole new light. The document he obtained on March 8 was not just an obscure memo on a few Saudi

---

*See Appendix H for DIA Analysis of "The Intelligence Impact of the Unauthorized Disclosure to Israel of the 'DOD Analysis of the Saudi Arabian Request to Purchase F-15 Fighter Aircraft'."

**See Appendix H.

Arabian air bases, as I had thought at first. It probably was the most comprehensive Defense Department summary of the military capabilities of Middle Eastern countries. It was a closely guarded document — the kind of document to which not even Israeli intelligence agents were allowed access.

The DIA's analysis confirmed that the document would have been of tremendous value to the Israelis, but so many portions of the analysis were blacked out that it did not say exactly what that value would be. Clearly, an intimate knowledge of the defense capabilities of the individual states in the region would benefit Israel. Israel's 1981 air strike against a nuclear reactor in Iraq provides one example of the value of such knowledge. France had been assisting in the development of the reactor, but when the project was finally nearing completion, Israeli jets struck and destroyed it. The most disturbing aspect of this attack was that Israeli jets were able to fly undetected through both Saudi Arabian and Jordanian airspace. Did the document in question enable the Israelis to find a seam in the Saudi radar defense system through which they flew on their way to Iraq? If so, would knowledge of the information contained in the document allow Israel to launch surprise attacks throughout the Middle East? Could Israel even attack U.S. allies and friends in the region, such as Saudi Arabia, Jordan and the Gulf States?

Since the Israeli air strike against the Iraqis did not take place until 1981, investigators working on the Bryen probe never had the opportunity to consider whether there was a connection. But the DIA analysis was enough to heighten my suspicions of Bryen.

My notes from the days of the investigation showed that Mahoney had called me on December 14, 1978, and said that he expected to wrap up the case within a month or so. That was about three weeks after he had received the DIA's analysis. Like me, Mahoney must have thought that it was no accident that Bryen had obtained the Pentagon document the day before his meeting with the Israelis. He probably thought that all the elements were there to advance the investigation to a grand jury: motive to help the Israelis; opportunity, in the form of the Madison meeting; a witness to Bryen's intent to give the Israelis the Pentagon document and an authoritative analysis concluding that the document was classified and was of great value to the Israelis.

The DIA analysis made it clear that Ron Stern was wrong when he told Heymann that the document Bryen may have offered was not a "document on the bases." There also was a difference of opinion as to whether the case would be "wrapped up," and if so, with what result. Stern, however, was correct in portraying Lisker as being suspicious of Bryen. Documents indicated that at about the same time Mahoney received the DIA's analysis, Lisker realized that Bryen needed to answer a lot of questions. A November 24, 1978, note from Davitt to Lisker said:

> Ron Stern called to say he has discussed the Bryen case with Phil Heymann, that Phil prefers the deposition option, and would like us to make immediate arrangements to take it.
>
> Will you please prepare a letter for me to sign to Lewin recalling his previous offer (to have Bryen take a deposition), etc.
>
> Phil would like to be kept posted if any problems develop in obtaining Bryen's cooperation.[31]

Davitt promptly sent a letter to Lewin to arrange for a deposition of Bryen. Lewin countered with three conditions: that he be present, that the Department provide, in writing, a list of areas of inquiries and that the Department set a date by which the investigation would be terminated.[32]

A month later, Davitt informed Lewin of the topics that he

and Lisker wanted to cover in the Bryen deposition.

AREAS TO BE COVERED IN THE INTERVIEW OF
STEPHEN D. BRYEN

1. Circumstances surrounding meeting with the Israelis on March 9, 1978 at Madison Hotel Coffee Shop, including specifics of conversations.

2. Details of Mr. Bryen's request for, access to, and/or utilization of certain classified information, specifically the following:

   (a) "DOD analysis of the Saudi Arabian request to purchase F-15 fighter aircraft," classified: "SECRET/NO FORN."

   (b) "Request for photographs of the Saudi base under construction at Tabuk, showing all facilities and communications and radar emplacements on the site and showing in outline any further planned expansion or deployment of equipment or material at the site."

   (c) Circumstances and subsequent actions regarding the May 1977 oral request at Aman, [sic] Jordan, for scale maps with Jordanian I-Hawk site locations plotted.

3. Details of relations with Israeli diplomats, officials, agents or employees 1977-78, both in the U.S. and abroad.

4. Details of relations with representatives or employees of any U.S. domestic lobbying organization supportive of Israel.[33]

As for Lewin's two other demands, Davitt agreed that Lewin could be present for the deposition; but said it was impossible for the Department to set a date for completion of the investigation since Bryen's answers might require additional inquiry.[34]

Lewin responded with a scathing letter criticizing the Department's investigation and refusing to permit Bryen to be interviewed without a guarantee that the matter would soon be resolved. Lewin, believing that the best defense was a strong offense, went on the attack:

> The individual who initiated this investigation had a patent political motive to "target" Mr. Bryen in order to incapacitate him on the staff of the Senate Foreign Relations Committee. This obvious bias should have been viewed as a reason for treating the entire matter expeditiously and determining quickly whether there was any substance to the particular charge he made . . .
>
> The two new subjects that you have now introduced (i.e., "relations with Israeli diplomats and domestic lobbying organizations") are an obvious means of harassing him by inquiring into areas as to which there is no shred of evidence of criminal conduct, but where inquiry would serve the interests of particular foreign powers. These foreign interests have announced publicly that they are pressuring the Department with regard to this investigation, and it is clear that the totally new direction in which you wish to point this investigation implements their purpose.[35]

Lewin really tried to turn the tables. Although it was his client who was being investigated, he said that it was I who had the "patent political motive" and the NAAA which was controlled by "foreign interests." The ferocity of his attack revealed how anxious he was to prevent the Justice Department from asking Bryen, under oath, about his relations with such foreign interests as the Israeli diplomats and agents.

Davitt and Lisker were not intimidated. They countered with the January 26, 1979 "Action Memorandum," and used the strongest possible language:

> The second option and the one which we urge strongly is to complete this important inquiry before an investigative grand jury. [Emphasis added.] Some of the unresolved questions thus far, which suggest that Bryen is (a) gathering classified information for the Israelis, (b) acting as their unregistered agent and (c) lying about it, are as follows: [Following five-and-one-half pages blacked out].36*

The Action Memorandum appeared to be the only document in which investigators compiled nearly all the evidence against Bryen.

While Lisker and Davitt wanted to continue on course, Philip Heymann, their boss, seemed more affected by Lewin's criticism. After receiving a carbon copy of Lewin's letter, which was sent directly to him, but before the Davitt action memo, Heymann sent a note to an assistant asking, "Should I get into this or stay out? Can we come to a decision one way or the other quickly? The Senate Foreign Relations Committee has now asked the White House to be promptly informed of any deposition. Will you see that this happens? Thanks."37

Ronald Stern, Heymann's personal assistant, was skeptical of the grand jury option. On January 26, 1979, as Davitt and Lisker prepared their recommendation, Stern wrote the following note to Heymann:

> Yesterday (1/25), I met with Jack Davitt, Joel Lisker and Ed Sharp (FBI) to discuss what our next step should be in view of the most recent letter from Nat Lewin. Jack & Joel (and presumably Ed) read the 1/17 letter as a

---

* See Appendix C.

final rejection of a deposition option and want to go to a grand jury stage. I remain skeptical toward that approach in this case and we discussed other options short of using a grand jury. We concluded that Jack and Joel should provide you both with a detailed memo explaining why they wanted to use a grand jury, why it would be appropriate in this case, and what they hoped to accomplish, and why other options were unsatisfactory. I will reserve judgment and comments until I receive a copy of their memo which they promised to forward in a couple of days.[38]

Heymann presumably shared Stern's "skepticism" about the need for a grand jury probe. Apparently he felt the Department should still have pursued the deposition option. He also must have felt there was too much animosity between Lewin, on the one hand, and Davitt and Lisker on the other. In the months following the Action Memorandum, Heymann instructed Deputy Assistant Attorney General Robert Keuch to handle contact with Lewin.

Keuch met with Lewin on March 5 to discuss again the possibility of a deposition. Lewin told Keuch he wanted to bar questions about Bryen's relations with the Israeli lobby and pressed Keuch for specifics about allegations against his client. Keuch refused to budge. A month later, Keuch called and proposed an "open-ended" interview with a preliminary explanation to each question at the time of the interview. Lewin refused to agree to this proposition.[39]

After a few months of useless bartering, Keuch realized that Lewin was not going to cooperate. He realized that Davitt and Lisker were right: the appropriate forum for questioning Bryen was the grand jury. In what could have been a key turning point in the investigation, Keuch wrote the following letter. Written on Heymann's letterhead [Assistant

Attorney General, Criminal Division], the letter authorized
Lisker to proceed with a grand jury probe. Dated May 25,
1979, it read:

> As an attorney for the Government employed full
> time by the Department of Justice and assigned to the
> Criminal Division, you are hereby authorized and
> directed to file information and to conduct in the
> District of Columbia and any other judicial district any
> kind of legal proceedings, civil or criminal, including
> grand jury proceedings before United States Magis-
> trates, which United States Attorneys are authorized
> to conduct.

> You may file a copy of this letter with the Clerk of
> the District Court to evidence this authorization.

> Sincerely,

> Philip B. Heymann
> Assistant Attorney General
> Criminal Division

> By: [Signature]
> Robert L. Keuch
> Deputy Assistant Attorney General
> (Pursuant to Order No. 725-77,
> dated May 12, 1977)[40]

Finally, it appeared that Lisker would get the opportunity to
question Bryen under oath about the discrepancies in his
stories, the facts surrounding his requests for U.S. military
secrets that were of interest to Israel, and his cozy relations
with Israeli officials and pro-Israeli lobbyists.

On May 31, Keuch informed Lewin that Heymann had
determined to proceed with a grand jury investigation. Lewin

quickly moved to reverse the decision. Lewin called Heymann on two consecutive days, June 7 and 8, and offered to make Bryen available for an interview on "the subjects covered in Paragraph 2 of Mr. Davitt's letter of December 27, 1978."[41] That paragraph concerned Bryen's access to DOD documents on the F-15 sale, the Tabuk base and the I-Hawk missiles. Lewin would still not allow Bryen to be questioned about his relations with Israeli agents or lobbyists, or even about the details of his conversation with the Israelis in the Madison. Lewin later described his key exchange with Heymann in a letter to Heymann:

> Given the earlier course of the investigation and Mr. Bryen's total cooperation with it, I believed that this [the grand jury probe] was a waste of government funds and energy and unjustifiably subjected Mr. Bryen to the obloquy of being a target of a grand jury proceeding. I spoke with you on the telephone on June 7 and 8. I offered at that time, on Mr. Bryen's behalf, to make him available for an interview on the subjects covered in Paragraph 2 of Mr. Davitt's letter of December 27, 1978, with no other conditions attached. I told you that I would be out-of-town during the first part of the week of June 11. I suggested that an interview could be conducted at the end of that week — June 14 or 15 — and that the Department of Justice attorney handling the matter (whom you identified as Joel Lisker, Esq.) could arrange a time and place with my office. *I understood from our conversation that Mr. Lisker would be instructed to proceed on that basis.* [Emphasis added].[42]

In other words, it appeared that after two phone calls from Lewin, Heymann reversed a major decision to go to the grand jury — a decision that had been a year in the making and had been recommended strongly by high-level staffers and concurred in by Keuch, the Deputy Assistant Attorney General of the Criminal Division. Moreover, Heymann agreed to Lewin's demands that investigators not be allowed to ask Bryen about his relations with Israeli officials or lobbyists.

Heymann's decision created a dilemma for Lisker. To make a case against Bryen, Lisker had to prove that he had actually disclosed classified data to the Israelis, and therefore violated U.S. espionage law, or acted on behalf of the Government of Israel, thereby breaching the Foreign Agents Registration Act. However, because Heymann agreed to Lewin's demands, Lisker could not question Bryen about his relations with Israeli agents. Thus, Lisker had been barred from pursuing an important avenue of inquiry in determining whether Bryen had violated the Foreign Agents Registration Act.

Given these restrictions, the only places to which Lisker could turn to gather the evidence he needed before interviewing Bryen were the Committee staffers and the files of the Senate Foreign Relations Committee. When Lisker and Davitt sought to interview several of the Committee staffers with whom FBI agents had spoken a year earlier, however, they learned that Patrick Shea, the new Committee counsel, objected to Heymann in a letter and demanded that he be present at all interviews. In a written reply, Heymann noted that Lisker had agreed to this demand.[43] Thus, while FBI agents interviewed Bryen's colleagues in complete privacy, Lisker had to interview them in the presence of the Committee's counsel. This undoubtedly had an effect on their willingness to speak freely. As *Defense Week* later reported, a "source close to the investigation" said the Justice Department, "did the interviews, but we had to talk to the staff people with the committee counsel present. There was a chilling effect. Recognizing the possiblity of a grand jury, some of them weren't as helpful as they'd been with the FBI."[44]

Likser also learned that the Committee wanted to control his access to its records. Senator Stone's desire to screen material before investigators could look at it caused further delays.[45] Meanwhile, Lewin kept calling to complain to Lisker about how long it was taking him to arrange the "final" interview with Bryen.[46] On August 16, Heymann made another important decision; he ordered Davitt and Lisker to proceed with the Bryen interview with or without the Committee's documents. "If additional evidence was received which was a basis to reopen the investigation, then it would be reopened," Lisker wrote in a memo recounting Heymann's instructions.[47]

Lisker called Lewin to arrange the interview with Bryen. When Lisker explained that an additional interview would probably be necessary after he had received the Committee documents, Lewin "expressed substantial doubt whether it made sense for Mr. Bryen to come in for a day-long fourth interview if it was probable that a fifth interview demand would follow."[48] They discussed the case and, according to Lewin, Lisker said that a detailed interview would be necessary since he could not understand why Bryen lied about things that were not important. Lewin pressed him for specifics. Finally, Lisker mentioned Bryen's denying that he could speak or understand Hebrew.

In a September 6, 1979 letter to Heymann, Lewin once again stated his opposition to a fourth interview of Bryen if another interview would be necessary. He also used the Hebrew issue to accuse the Department of trying to set a "perjury trap" for Bryen.

> This allegation was absolutely incredible! After more than a year of hiding its cards and playing Junior Detective with the life and career of an outstanding, sincere, dedicated, loyal and assiduous public servant,

the Department of Justice had come forth with an allegation so spurious and so hollow that I was left momentarily speechless.

> . . . . I am appalled and outraged at the conduct of the Department of Justice in this investigation . . . . You may now proceed in whatever manner you choose with this outrageous witchhunt, but you can no longer count on any cooperation from my client or from me.[49]

Lisker still would not give up. He seemed to think that the Senate Foreign Relations Committee had something in its files, and he wanted to see them. Committee Counsel Shea insisted on erecting additional roadblocks. He argued that Lisker should not have blanket access to Committee files because it would violate the constitutional separation of the executive and legislative branches. Shea proposed to permit Senator Case, Bryen and Lewin to review the Committee files and assert a privilege for any that Case and Bryen may have authored. Lisker opposed the procedure, saying it violated the Committee's pledge to cooperate with the investigation and allow access to its employees and records. Futher, Lisker told Shea:

> . . . . the Committee was affording Bryen a special privilege which should not be given to subjects of criminal investigations, and that, in this instance, it would put us in a most difficult position since our review was designed to obtain information with which to question Bryen. This review gives him the opportunity to anticipate possible questions and concoct responses.[50]*

Despite Lisker's objections, Case, Lewin and Bryen were

---

*See Appendix H

permitted to screen the documents. A month later, Lisker still had not been afforded that opportunity and called Shea. He asked if Case, Lewin or Bryen wanted to bar Lisker's review of any documents. "He hesitated several seconds before responding, and then said while he would answer my question this time, in the future he would not feel bound to do so. He then went on to say that Lewin did identify certain documents for which he recommended a 'speech or debate' privilege should be claimed if I requested that they be turned over to the Department."[51]*

It appeared that Heymann did not think that the review of the Committee's files was worth waiting for. On October 10, nearly a month before Lisker was permitted to see the Committee files, an unidentified Department official wrote a routing slip to Bob Keuch, stating, "PBH wants to close this —Joel will get letter to Lewin telling him." "PBH" was Philip B. Heymann and "Joel" was Lisker.[52]

On October 15, Davitt prepared the "closing" memo in the Bryen case which he had promised Heymann a few days earlier. "A letter to Nat Lewin informing him of our decision will be forthcoming in the next few days," Davitt told Heymann.[53]

A month later, in his final memo to Davitt, a frustrated Lisker described how Shea, two days earlier, finally allowed him to inspect some of the Committee's documents.

> I have now completed the review of the documents which were culled, by Shea, from Committee files pursuant to our letter of request dated August 6. The documents which I was permitted to review had a measured thickness of approximately 4 inches. They had been extracted from a full file drawer of documents

---

*See Appendix I for Memorandum of Joel S. Lisker to Files, October 23, 1979.

by Shea.

The review disclosed several documents which clearly indicate that Bryen was furnishing information to the Israeli Defense Ministry. I have attached a reconstructed copy of one such document which was transcribed from my notes. The files which I reviewed failed to disclose that any classified documents were furnished to the Israelis by Bryen or that Bryen acted as an agent of the Government of Israel. The attachment does corroborate statements by several witnesses who were aware of Bryen's peculiar relationship with Israeli Government officials, but who were unable to establish that he had furnished classified information.

Based on the foregoing, it appears that the case should remain closed.[54]

Lisker's frustration was understandable. In January 1979, he and Davitt had written the Action Memorandum strongly urging grand jury action, and suggesting that Bryen was acting as an Israeli agent and lying about it. But in October 1979, the Justice Department, without ever taking Bryen's deposition, without going to the grand jury and without yet obtaining the Senate documents, decided to close the case.

The Justice Department's file gave a fairly detailed picture of the Bryen investigation. Yet as Assistant Attorney General Robert McConnell wrote to Associate Attorney General Rudolph Giuliani, "there were a number of unanswered questions regarding Bryen's relationship with officials of the Israeli Government and in particular his efforts to obtain sensitive information for which he had no apparent legitimate need but which would have been of inestimable value to the Israelis. . ."[55] To ensure that no stone was left unturned, I worked with journalists and researchers to interview Justice Department officials involved in the investigation and to retrace the steps they took in its early days.

None of the Justice or FBI investigators would discuss the details of the investigation itself, nor did they want to be quoted by name about anything remotely connected with it. Joel Lisker, who was now staff director of the Senate Judiciary Subcommittee on Terrorism, was the only one who was still in Washington. The others had moved elsewhere to take new jobs. They expressed concern that Bryen was permitted to take a high-level job in the Pentagon. "I was watching television one night," explained one investigator, "when Bryen came on the screen. I almost fell out of my chair when I saw he was the Deputy Assistant Secretary of Defense. How in the world could they have let that happen?"[56]

Another investigator also expressed surprise that Bryen was able to land the Defense Department job. Although careful not to tell us anything about the investigation that we did not already know, he said, "Keep pursuing it and you will have a very interesting story!"[57]

"The Bryen case was an unusual one in many ways," said a third source who worked on the case. "Most of the time we can determine whether or not a suspect was guilty or innocent. Not so with Bryen. We could never prove that he did leak classified data, but we never proved to our satisfaction that he didn't do it either. He kept telling us things that were contradicted by evidence we learned later. This increased our suspicions. There's a maxim for law enforcers: 'False in one, false in all.' But after a year-and-a-half, the investigation ran out of steam. We had to close it with many, many unanswered questions."[58]

We then approached many of the people who worked with Bryen on the Senate Foreign Relations Committee. Many were reluctant to discuss the case. However, nearly all said that Bryen was an outspoken supporter of Israel who did not trust those not sharing his views. "At times you wondered, if he had to choose between Israel and the United States, which one he'd choose," said one staffer.[59]

"He was pretty well plugged into the Israeli network," said another former staffer.[60]

Most of Bryen's former colleagues did not say he was unpleasant or difficult to get along with. He simply had strong feelings about Israel and did not hide them. He was not at all discreet.

What seemed to trouble some staffers the most about Bryen was his relationship with the Israeli Embassy. Zvi Rafiah, a counselor at the Israeli Embassy, was in regular contact with Bryen. Rafiah visited him in his Senate staff office as many as three times a week, according to one source. He made full use of the office phones and at times would spend many hours there.[61]

Bryen's office was near the Committee safe in which classified material was kept. Rafiah, on more than one occasion, was in the office with Bryen when the safe door was wide open. One source said Bryen and Rafiah regularly spoke to each other in a "foreign language which sounded like Hebrew." Another source said the two were overheard having what sounded like a heated argument in Hebrew.[62]

"At times they gave you the impression that Rafiah was in charge and Bryen was the good soldier," a source said.[63]

Other staffers said they were not surprised that Bryen was accused of offering classified data to the Israelis because they had their own suspicions. What surprised them was that Bryen was indiscreet enough to focus attention on his special relationship. All of these sources said that they told the FBI agents about Bryen's reputation for being pro-Israel and his close relationship with Rafiah. Despite their suspicions of Bryen, no one we spoke with actually saw him hand over secret material to the Israelis.[64]

The Bryen investigation spurred great interest among the staffers and many rumors about what the FBI had found out. Key staffers believed the FBI had found evidence with which to indict Bryen. "The gossip in the corridor," said one source, "was that the FBI had the goods to give Bryen a very hard time, but didn't use it because they did not want to reveal their methods of obtaining it."[65]

The FBI and the Justice Department had plenty of circumstantial evidence suggesting, as Davitt had said, that Bryen was acting as an Israeli agent. The key to making full use of the circumstantial evidence was to question Bryen and other witnesses under oath, preferably before a grand jury. Nathan Lewin understandably wanted to keep his client out of this predicament. Lewin pressed Heymann not to honor his subordinates' call for a grand jury. He also asked Heymann to agree to exclude questions about relations with Israeli agents and lobbyists. It all led us back to a familiar question: Did Heymann go along? I realized that I needed to know more about Heymann. I also needed to learn more about Lewin. What I soon discovered made everything easier to understand.

Philip B. Heymann was named Assistant Attorney General in charge of the Criminal Division in 1978, shortly after the FBI began its investigation of Bryen. Benjamin R. Civiletti, his predecessor, had replaced Griffen Bell as Attorney General. Heymann was a Harvard Law professor, a member of the Watergate prosecutor's team and a U.S. Air Force veteran, with an impressive resume. In sum, a straight arrow with an impeccable reputation.

Nathan Lewin was equally accomplished. He also had served in the Justice Department, and had been a Law professor at Harvard and Georgetown Universities. Lewin was an active supporter of Israel and had represented members of the Jewish Defense League. If being indiscreet at the Madison Hotel that fateful day was the dumbest thing

Stephen Bryen ever did, then the smartest thing he did to avoid the consequences of his mistake was going to Nathan Lewin. Lewin's experience was impressive, and his commitment to Israel was unquestioned. More importantly, he and Phil Heymann were close friends, and had known each other for twenty years.

According to one source, Heymann came to Washington in 1978 to assume his new job, but did not yet have a place to live. He looked up his old friend Nat Lewin who took him in as a houseguest for a while. An investigator who worked on the Bryen case said, "We knew that Phil and Nat were friends, but we did not appreciate the depth of their friendship."[66]

Another source who knew them both said, "Sure they were friends. And if anyone else was involved I would be suspicious myself. But Phil Heymann is a man of such integrity that he wouldn't let his friendship with Lewin interfere with his professional judgment. Hell, Lewin used to complain that he couldn't lobby Phil on the Bryen case when they went to the theatre together because it wouldn't have been proper."[67] But Lewin had the kind of ready access to the head of the Justice Department's Criminal Division that most lawyers representing criminal suspects do not enjoy.

A look at their careers reveals the roots of their friendship. Heymann left the Air Force in 1957 to go to Harvard Law School. He was case editor of the *Harvard Law Review* between 1957-1960. Lewin was editor of the *Harvard Law Review* from 1958-1959, and its treasurer from 1959-1960.

After finishing third in his class, Heymann become a law clerk to Supreme Court Justice John M. Harlan and retained this position until August 1961. Lewin clerked for Justice Harlan in 1961-1962. Meanwhile, Heymann went to work as a lawyer in the Justice Department's Office of Solicitor General from 1961-1965. In 1963, Lewin became an Assistant to the Solicitor General and stayed until 1967.

The pattern continued. In 1965, Heymann went to the State Department's Bureau of Security and Consular Affairs to become deputy administrator. Between 1966-1967 he was acting administrator. In 1967, Lewin came on board as deputy administrator. In 1968, Heymann returned to Harvard to teach law. Lewin was a visiting professor at Harvard in 1974-1975.[68]

It seemed, career-wise, that Heymann, who was four years older than Lewin, led the way like an older brother. Lewin followed faithfully, taking employment where Heymann had been before Heymann moved on to something else. Given the closeness of their friendship, should Heymann have taken himself out of the case?

Lewin's complaints about Pletcher's aggressive style with Bryen had prompted the Justice Department's Office of Professional Responsibility to refer the matter to the Inspection Division of the FBI, which conducted a brief investigation of the FBI agent and decided that the matter did not warrant further attention. The Office of Professional Responsibility, however, never was alerted to the personal relationship between Lewin and Heymann, and consequently never examined the impact, if any, it might have on the Bryen investigation.

The documents clearly showed that Heymann made the key decisions to terminate the investigation of Bryen. In January 1979, he rejected his staff's recommendation of a grand jury probe. Five months later, when he decided to follow his staff's recommendation, he changed his mind after two phone calls from Nathan Lewin. It was even harder to understand why Heymann agreed to Lewin's demand that Bryen not be asked about his relations with Israeli officials or domestic lobbyists. Since when does an Assistant Attorney General of the United States agree to a line of questioning demanded by the lawyer representing a man who is being investigated for espionage and violations of the Foreign Agents Registration Act?

The Watergate years emphasized the prinicple that the United States was a system of laws, not of men. The laws at issue in the Bryen case were the Espionage Act [18 U.S.C. 793] and the Foreign Agents Registration Act [22 U.S.C. 612]. The Espionage Act:

> Makes it a crime for anyone, with intent or reason to believe that it is to be used to the injury of the United States, or to the advantage of a foreign nation, to receive or to obtain, or communicate, deliver, transmit, or attempt to receive, obtain, communicate, deliver or transmit to any foreign government, or any representative, officer or agent, employee or citizen thereof, either directly or indirectly, any document, writing, photograph or information relating to the national defense. The penalty for violation is death or imprisonment for any term of years or for life.

The Foreign Agents Registration Act:

> Requires any person who acts as an agent of a foreign government to register with the Attorney General. The Act defines an agent of a foreign government as any person who acts as an agent, representative employee or servant or who acts in any other capacity at the order, request, or under the direction or control of a foreign principal or of a person any of whose activities are directly or indirectly supervised, directed, controlled, financed or subsidized in whole or in part by a foreign principal, and who, directly or through any person
>
> 1. engages within the United States in political activities for or in the interests of any such foreign principal;

2. acts within the United States as a public relations counsel, publicity agent, information service employee, or political consultant for, or in the interests of, such foreign principal;

3. within the United States solicits, collects, disperses, or dispenses contributions, loans, money or other things of value in the interests of such foreign principal; or

4. within the United States represents the interests of such foreign principal before any agency or official of the Government of the United States.

Of course, laws are merely words on paper. To have meaning they must be respected and enforced — by people and governments. In the Bryen case, several Justice Department officials who believed in our American system of laws worked hard to see those laws enforced. They wanted to take the investigation as far as necessary to achieve justice and ensure that nobody would feel they could so easily hand over our nation's secrets to foreigners, regardless of what country was involved. But these officials did not get their way. Their recommendations for a thorough grand jury investigation of Bryen were not heeded by Phil Heymann.

The investigation was closed before a conclusive end was reached. The threat of prosecution was lifted, and Bryen was free to pursue a career in which he could enjoy greater access to more of America's most sensitive classified military data.

CHAPTER 7

A PERLE WITH STRINGS

My lengthy examination of the Bryen investigation led me to the bitterly disappointing conclusion that Bryen had slipped away despite substantial evidence that the case should have gone to a grand jury. In the final analysis, Bryen never had to answer for his conduct, despite the efforts of conscientious Justice Department and FBI investigators. Nathan Lewin, using his vital contacts and powers of persuasion, was able to prevent a grand jury probe of his client.

What I learned should have been enough to generate renewed press interest in Bryen's past. However, it was obvious the media's main concern was the present. Bryen's past was interesting, but it was now 1983 — five years since the Madison incident. The only way I could spread awareness about the potential threats posed by Bryen was to focus on his present activities in the Defense Department. This would be a difficult task for several reasons. The lessons of the past clearly would have taught him to be more discrete. Moreover, his Defense Department post enabled him to work behind the curtain of secrecy that traditionally protects defense and national security policymaking.

While Bryen seemed to avoid the limelight as much as possible, Assistant Secretary of Defense Richard Perle, who had appointed Bryen to his Defense Department position, was much more visible. Supposedly, they both were working on issues relating to NATO policy, East-West relations and technology transfer — not the Middle East. Policy toward Israel and the Arab states was supposed to be handled by other branches of the Defense Department, the State Department and the White House.

On occasion, however, news reports surfaced suggesting that Perle kept a hand in Middle East issues. Late in 1981, for instance, *Air Force* magazine, quoting Perle and intelligence sources, reported that Israeli jets killed eleven Soviets in Lebanon when they destroyed one of their own downed aircraft to prevent highly secret equipment from falling into enemy hands.

The article said that Perle "recently disclosed that the Israeli Air Force lost an aircraft carrying highly secret Israeli developed ECM [electronic counter-measures] equipment," and that the Israelis, "determined not to let the equipment fall into enemy hands, mounted a strike to destroy totally the downed aircraft on the ground." Perle was also quoted as saying that, by the time the Israelis got to the wreckage, there were "already Russians on the ground pulling out pieces" and that, as a result, the Israelis "got the Russians" as well as the downed plane.[1]

Perle also emerged as an opponent of the planned Kuwaiti take-over of Sante Fe International Corp., an American firm specializing in oil drilling equipment, which was up for sale. Kuwait is an Arab state, and Perle said there were "national security aspects" about the deal because a Sante Fe subsidiary, D.F. Braun & Co., had performed important design and engineering work on the Department of Energy's nuclear weapons plants at Rocky Flats, Colorado, and at the Hanford Reservation in Washington state. A company spokesman said Perle was exaggerating since Braun's nuclear work was only a small fraction of the company's business and had nothing to do with weaponry.

Perle intervened after the Department of Energy said it would not object to the Kuwaiti take-over. In a letter to Representative Benjamin Rosenthal, a New York Democrat and ardent supporter of Israel, Perle said, "We have to balance the security arrangements administered by the Department of Energy against the possibility these arrangements could prove inadequate and might lead to untoward results in the Persian Gulf region." Perle was a member of the interagency Committee on Foreign Investment in the United States, which Rosenthal had asked to investigate the Sante Fe sale.[2]

I needed to find out more about Richard Perle and his policies. I learned that he, like other high-level U.S. Government officials, was required to file detailed statements of his income, former employment and assets to certify that in his official duties there would be "no actual or potential conflict of interest." Perle had been late in filing his "conflict of interest" forms.

In February 1983, however, forms filed by Perle indicated that in 1980 he received substantial consulting fees from the Abington Corporation, TRW, Northrop, System Development Corporation and Tamares Ltd. I decided to send the information to Jeff Gerth, a *New York Times* investigative reporter specializing in defense matters.

On Sunday, April 17, 1983, Gerth broke a front page story which gave Perle something to which he was not accustomed: negative publicity. The story centered on Perle's connection with the Israelis.

> Richard N. Perle, an Assistant Secretary of Defense, recommended that the Army consider buying weapons from an Israeli Company a year after he accepted a $50,000 consulting fee from the company's owners, according to Mr. Perle and an attorney for the weapons dealer.

Mr. Perle, the Assistant Secretary for International Security Policy, one of the most influential policy-makers in the Pentagon, acknowledged in interviews that he received the consulting fee the same month he entered the Government in 1981. He also acknowledged that in his official capacity he wrote a memorandum to the Secretary of the Army urging evaluation of the Israeli company's weapons.[3]

Gerth's story explored the complex network of names and companies behind Perle's questionable dealings. The key players appeared to be Shlomo Zabludowicz and his son Chaim. Shlomo Zabludowicz, who lived near Tel Aviv, Israel, was the founder and principal shareholder of Soltam Ltd, an Israeli company that manufactured mortars, artillery, ammunition and other military as well as civilian products. He also founded a Liechtenstein-based company called Etablissements Salgad, to hold patents on mortars and act as an international sales agent. Tamares Ltd. was a wholly owned subsidiary of Salgad and was based in London. Pocal Industries, a Pennsylvania manufacturing plant, was set up by the Zabludowiczes in September 1981 to buy the patent rights to various mortar training rounds and to manufacture them. The story followed the money.

The . . . Zabludowiczes became clients of Mr. Perle in 1980. They paid $90,000 to the Abington Corporation, a consulting company where Mr. Perle worked that was owned by John F. Lehman Jr., now the Secretary of the Navy.

It was not until January 1982, nine months after Mr. Perle says the Zabludowiczes stopped being his clients, that he settled his financial arrangements with Mr. Lehman and Abington and received a portion of the $90,000 fee from 1980. The $50,000 Mr. Perle received in March 1981 was in addition to his share of the Abington fee.

The $140,000 in payments to Mr. Perle and Abington were channeled through Tamares. The company's certified annual report filed in London shows Tamares to be a tiny, unprofitable company, with total assets of less than $25,000 and sales of $250,000 for the year ended 1982. Mr. Spiegel (the Zabludowiczes' lawyer) said the consulting fees originated with other Zabludowicz companies, although Mr. Perle reported receiving the $50,000 from Tamares.

Spiegel . . . said his clients had hired Mr. Perle as part of a strategy to gain a toehold in marketing various weapons and ammunition to the Defense Department.

The Zabludowiczes want to wrest from the British a contract for supplying mortars to the United States Army. The contract is potentially worth hundreds of millions of dollars. So far the Zabludowiczes have been unsuccessful, but several other bids by their companies are still under review within the Defense Department.

Mr. Perle said his real value to the Zabludowiczes had been in devising a "strategy" for them. He said he was friends with his former clients and still talked with them occasionally about their business dealings.4

Perle got involved in the deal in 1982 when Senator William Cohen of Maine asked the Army to evaluate the cost competitiveness of the Soltam mortar manufactured by the Israelis. Perle disagreed with a reply by Army Secretary John O. Marsh which essentially endorsed the British product currently under contract rather than the Israeli one. Perle wrote a memo to Marsh, arguing that the Army had not given the Israeli mortar a fair testing, and added, "I am familiar with the documented and systematic suppression of the Tampella mortar, undertaken in the last Administration to shield the UK 81 from competition, because the Tampella marketing organization was a client of mine."

Tampella was a Finnish conglomerate that originally designed the mortars and then licensed them to Shlomo Zabludowicz, who was a former Tampella official. Soltam later manufactured the Tampella-type mortar while Zabludowicz's other company, Salgad, marketed it.

The Army honored Perle's request and re-evaluated the Israeli mortar, but rejected it after concluding that the Israeli offer was not cost-effective. The Zabuldowiczes had three other bids pending at the Pentagon. "Mr. Perle said he did not recall involving himself in the other Soltam procurement matters pending within the Pentagon. Mr. Perle acknowledged that he might not have properly filled out the 1982 financial disclosure statement he was required to file with the Office of Government Ethics."[5]

The same day the story broke, Perle appeared on NBC's "Meet the Press." In response to questions about the *New York Times* story, Perle said he had not felt it necessary to disqualify himself from the Soltam bid because "the ultimate issue, of course, was a question of procurement, and I am not a procurement officer." Perle also said the "prominence" and "length" of the front page article was "out of all proportion to the events that it purports to describe." Perle did not dispute any of the facts in the article.[6]

Perle's nonchalant attitude was quite a change from his reaction a few days earlier when he learned the *New York Times* was going to run Gerth's story. Perle reportedly attempted to get the *Times* Washington bureau to kill the story. When that did not work, he called on well-placed friends to make an effort to get the New York editors to remove it.[7] The move backfired. The story was originally scheduled to run on a Friday, but Perle's efforts delayed it until Sunday, the day he was scheduled to appear on "Meet the Press."

The Gerth article also reported that Perle had taken $5,000 from TRW, another defense contractor, and that Perle's title of Assistant Secretary was deceiving.

> Mr. Perle's influence in the Reagan Administration far exceeds that normally held by an Assistant Secretary of Defense. In the transition, he was able to place associates in important national security positions and, in the Defense Department, he has played a major role in creating policies on arms control and trade with the Soviet Union.[8]

Newspapers quickly condemned Perle's actions. *The St. Louis Post-Dispatch* said that Perle's work on behalf of the Israeli mortar seller, "should be thoroughly investigated. Mr. Perle may have done nothing legally wrong, but there is most certainly a strong indication of indiscretion."[9]

The New York Times charged that Perle's conduct "falls beneath the standard set by other government officials, who disqualify themselves from matters involving former clients or employers."[10]

The *Boston Globe* declared the behavior "flunks" Pentagon rules on conflict of interests and "it surely offends the sensibilities of citizens who would not accept such conduct with equanimity in ordinary life." Citing a *Time* magazine story, the *Globe* also challenged Perle for sabotaging arms control initiatives and concluded, "Now thanks to Perle's misjudgment on the Israeli mortar question, and to *Time's* fine analysis of the Administration's negotiating strategy, citizens can put two and two together and see what makes the Reagan Pentagon purr."[11]

The Wall Street Journal ran a front page story expressing

concern about Perle's actions,[12] and United Press International reported, "The White House is reviewing allegations that Asst. Secretary of Defense Richard Perle intervened in an Army procurement matter on behalf of Israeli arms manufacturers that formerly employed him as a consultant, a spokesman said Monday. Deputy press secretary Peter Roussel said the White House counsel's office and 'possibly others' in the Administration were reviewing the allegations."[13]

CHAPTER 8

ALL IN THE FAMILY

Richard Perle proved that he could make his military expertise and allegiance to Israel pay handsomely. Although his questionable dealings received some criticism and unwelcome attention, no one posed a serious challenge or threat to his position.

Richard Perle, moreover, was just one component of the Perle family network. His wife, Leslie Barr, shared her husband's policy views. In October 1981, Barr was appointed to a high-level Commerce Department position and in late 1981 and early 1982, helped to develop a Reagan Administration plan to force U.S. oil companies to stop operations in Libya, an Arab country of North Africa. The two-tier plan called first for a bar on United States personnel doing business in Libya, and second for a total embargo on United States purchase of Libyan oil, as well as Libyan purchase of American oilfield equipment or other high technology products.[1]

According to a Commerce Department source, Barr directed a study in early 1982 that pronounced Libyan oil imports a "risk to U.S. national security interests." The study was contradicted by a later assessment carried out by the Congressional General Accounting Office, but the Libyan oil embargo was imposed nonetheless and a multi-billion dollar market was lost to American business.[2]

Leslie Barr maintained a low profile. When she first took

the Commerce Department position, several calls were placed to determine in which office she worked. Several Commerce Department officials, including some that had overlapping jurisdictions with Barr, said they had never heard of her.

Barr's husband, Richard Perle, however, has played a major, influential role in the Defense Department in terms of both policy and personnel. It was Perle who ensured that Bryen was brought safely on board at the Defense Department. He told Senators there was nothing in the Justice Department file that would raise questions about the propriety of Bryen holding a position which would allow him to see sensitive military data. I could see now that Perle had issued several misleading statements in response to the Senators' questions about Bryen. The Perle-Bryen alliance was exceedingly clear, and the connections between them, their policies, and an array of people in and out of the government became more and more obvious as I examined the FBI investigation of Bryen and the policies which he was eager to enact as Deputy Assistant Secretary of Defense.

According to a report by Bryen's office in the Defense Department, a major policy goal was to restrict the transfer of U.S. technology to "unfriendly" nations, a topic to which I would turn my energies in the months to come. The report also said that a primary means of enforcing this policy would be a new Customs Department program called "Project Exodus." The program called for stepped-up search and seizures by Customs Agents at major U.S. ports so exports would be more closely monitored. As the report explained,

> The Department of Defense has provided major support to this project in the form of a Congressionally approved one-time transfer in early 1982 of $30 million from the Defense Department to the Customs Service to fund expanded shipment inspection oper-

ations. Additionally, the Department of Defense has advised the Customs Service on types of equipment the Soviets are seeking and has provided materials for use by inspectors indicating ways that items of greatest military concern can be readily identified.

Defense believes enforcement efforts are a vital component of technology transfer control and intends to continue making available to appropriate enforcement agencies such information and advice as may be helpful.[3]

It seemed that the advice may have included suggestions about personnel changes. The Customs Department, on the bureaucratic flow chart, is a component of the Treasury Department and is overseen by Treasury's international division. In 1983, Leslie Barr dropped out of sight at the Commerce Department and reappeared as the director of the Customs Service International Program Management Division. It made us wonder if technology transfer controls required similar controls on personnel transfers.

Meanwhile, Bryen's wife, Shoshana Bryen, was holding the fort at the Jewish Institute for National Security Affairs. She had taken over as Executive Director and editor of the JINSA newsletter in the summer of 1981, after her husband had moved on to the Pentagon. Shoshana Bryen had a background in journalism, and it showed: the newsletter had improved greatly since she took charge, as she spruced up the format and eliminated errors.

Mrs. Bryen also got some editorial help. Leon Sloss, Frank Hoeber and Forrest Frank were added as contributing editors. Also featured on the JINSA Board of Advisors was Marvin Klemow, the Washington representative of Israeli Aircraft Industries.

The goals of the JINSA newsletter remained the same:

advocate strategic cooperation between the United States and Israel, including massive increases in U.S. aid and larger defense budgets; call for tough policies against the Soviets; deny the integrity of our Arab allies in the Middle East.

The newsletter was denser — filled with long stories and technical information about weapons, budgets and vital developments in the Middle East. The information it reported was, at times, impressive. But the newsletter did not always attribute the data to particular sources. For instance, in July 1981, after Israeli jets destroyed the Iraqi reactor, the JINSA newsletter ran an in-depth analysis of the construction of the reactor and Saudi Arabia's role in it. The story led with the following "Editor's Note" which indicated the Israeli Air Force may have found a seam in the Saudi and Jordanian air defense radar system.

On the afternoon of Sunday, 7 June, eight F-16 and six F-15 aircraft took off from an Israeli Air Force base. Each of the F-16s carried two general purpose 2000 lb. HE bombs. The F-15s provided air cover. The aircraft flew low over the southern part of Jordan into Saudi Arabia's northern tip straight to the Iraqi reactor site. The aircraft did not stay in the area more than 2 minutes. There was only scarce and inaccurate fire from the Iraqis, which did not affect the mission.

In the bombing run the Air Force destroyed the main structure of the Iraqi Osiraq reactor, a military-oriented underground construction site, and auxiliary installations. Neither the Soviet 2 MW or the French 1 MW research reactors on the site were hit since Israel declared it was after the "weapon" reactor and not the Iraqi nuclear research program.

The bombs fell at 6:30 PM Israel time (11:30 AM EST) with the aircraft coming in from the sun. After completing the raid, the fighters climbed and hurried back to Israel. They landed safely and the threat was removed.[4]

On the opposite page, a JINSA editorial claimed, "The question of the hour is not really whether or not Israel acted in self-defense by blowing up the Iraqi atomic reactor. The question is, rather, where the responsibility lies for creating that necessity, or minimally the perception of that necessity."[5]

On the same page, another JINSA editorial praised the Israeli's Merkhava tank and called for faster production of the M-1 tank. Soltam, the company owned by the Zabludowiczes who paid Perle $140,000, manufactured the gunnery systems for the Merkhava tank.[6]

JINSA's ultimate hope for strategic cooperation between Israel and the United States came true briefly in November 1981, when the two countries signed a "Memorandum of Understanding." The "MOU" called for increases in U.S. aid, the placing of advance U.S. facilities in Israel and technology transfers, just as Bryen had advocated a few years earlier. To JINSA's dismay, the MOU was suspended by Reagan when Israel annexed the Syrian Golan Heights. In its November 1982 issue, the JINSA newsletter bemoaned Reagan's action and posed its argument on the need for a U.S.-Israeli alliance to combat what it saw as a Russian-Radical Arab axis. "Suspension or cancellation" of the MOU, it said, "is not in the interest of the U.S. or Israel, but only of the Soviet Union." The article continued:

> The U.S. must keep its sights firmly on its strategic interests, which go beyond swipes at a friend. President Reagan has long been rightly convinced that the Soviet Union is at the heart of regional turmoil, and this is no time for him to let a disagreement on what is essentially a peripheral issue turn his attention away

from the primary problem . . . .

Israel's application of civil law to the Golan Heights hardly changes the face of the region. There was never a peace process there to be threatened by the move; there was never an indication of Syrian willingness to negotiate. In fact, well before the annexation there was an increase in the size, sophistication and organization of the Syrian Armed Force — which gave the appearance of a war waiting to happen.

Criticism can be leveled at Israel for timing, failure to consult its most important friend, stridency, emotionalism and any one of a number of things. However, punishment in the form of suspending the Memorandum of Understanding, and pique in cancelling it, are luxuries neither side can afford to indulge in. The MOU was not meant to be contingent on either side's performing services, and should have held a place of importance above political differences. As the Soviets continue to make political and military advances in the Middle East, the U.S. and Israel must return to their common interest.[7]

The JINSA newsletter also provided annual, detailed coverage of Reagan's proposed defense budget. While many experts criticized the budgets as a central cause of federal deficits and a threat to the U.S. economy, JINSA welcomed the huge increases year after year.

The defense budget is large and growing. But the defense effort of our principal adversary, the Soviet Union, is growing more rapidly, and has been for at least the past two decades. Furthermore, it is apparent that the Soviet Union is flexing its newly-found muscle to influence and coerce others, including allies and friends of the U.S.

Historically, democracies tend to relax their defense efforts when there is no war. The United States has done this. Now we are paying the price of attempting to play catch up. Few doubt that catching up is necessary . . . .

Can we afford the cost? A nation as large and wealthy as the United States must be able to allocate 6 or 7% of its GNP to its own defense, if a small state such as Israel spends almost 50% of its GNP for this purpose.[8]

In the months following the Israeli invasion of Lebanon, Joseph Churba, President of the Center for International Security, said that Israel's outstanding performance in defeating the PLO and Syrian forces proved that Israel was ready to stand on its own militarily. "Israel is now in a position to do whatever it wants," Churba stated: "Israeli power is not derivative from the United States today."[9]

Shoshana Bryen felt compelled to respond to Churba's assertion. In August 1982, she wrote an article for *Jewish Weekly* stating:

Israel and the U.S. have a complex military and political relationship, and to suggest that the outcome of Operation Peace for Galilee [invasion of Lebanon] alters the basic nature of the military side ignores reality. Israel buys an enormous quantity of material and spare parts, largely financed by U.S. grants and loans. Some French and British equipment aside, nearly all of Israel's arms purchases have come from the U.S. under our Foreign Military Sales (FMS) program.

According to Churba, the U.S. could save hundreds of millions, perhaps billions of dollars by tapping into

Jewish technological genius as represented by Israeli improvements in U.S. equipment. These are emotionally laden words, of which the Jewish community in particular should be wary . . . . They could translate into an erroneous suggestion that the only U.S. interest in Israel is the extraction of what it needs. This first of all denigrates the quiet but effective lines of communication already in place between the U.S. and Israel for the exchange of information . . . .[10]

Shoshana Bryen did not specify what "quiet but effective lines of communication between Israel and the U.S." existed, nor did she say who was on either end of the line.

In the following months, the JINSA newsletter concentrated heavily on the vital role technology played in Israel's defeat of Syrian and Palestinian forces during the 1982 invasion of Lebanon. In a November 1982 analysis, Frank Hoeber cited Israel's new "Scout," a remote-controlled model airplane, as a central reason for Israel's full control of the air space over Lebanon. Manufactured by Elta, a subsidiary of Israeli Aircraft Industries, the Scout acted as inexpensive "eyes and ears" for Israeli fighter jets without exposing pilots to enemy anti-aircraft fire. The nose of the mini-airplane contains a television camera which by relaying current views of Syrian surface-to-air missile sites to the so-called E-2C, a U.S. Navy-developed early warning and control aircraft, facilitated coordinated artillery and air attacks on the sites. The Scout also provided up-to-the-minute damage assessments which allowed attackers to avoid wasteful "overkill" and move on to additional sites.[11] The Scout was fundamentally responsible for Israel's success in destroying Syrian surface-to-air missile batteries in Lebanon.

Consisting mostly of epoxy, the Scout weighs 260 pounds,

has a wing span of 11 feet and is propelled by an 18-horsepower engine.[12] "The heart of the Scout," wrote Hoeber, "is the impressively compact electronic unit that not only contains the communications for guidance of the plane and return of information but also generates false radar images (electronic countermeasures, or ECM) that caused the SAMs to turn on their radars, thus confirming their positions to the Israeli-manned radars. This did not permit the Soviets successfully to attack the Scouts, which are built almost entirely of composites, and have a small gasoline engine mounted on top of the craft . . . and therefore have a very low radar cross-section, or signature visible to the ground radars."[13]

Thus one of the most important advances made by the Israeli military in preparation for the Lebanon invasion was the Scout, which, as Hoeber indicated, involved pioneering use of very-high-speed integrated circuits (VHSIC). It was VHSIC which made possible the creation of a communications relay device small enough to fit on a model airplane and fast enough to beam vital, timely intelligence data back to Israeli bombers.

The E-2C early warning radar aircraft also used the Scouts to monitor Syrian jets as they took off, thereby enabling Israeli fighters to launch the first air-to-air missiles "beyond visual range." This was further evidence of impressive Israeli use of American-developed very-high-speed integrated circuitry. The most impressive numbers were the final ones: the Israelis scored an 80-1 victory, according to Hoeber, with only one Israeli jet lost to "ground fire."[14]

It might have been a coincidence, but Stephen Bryen, who had become a leading player in the Pentagon's new program to control technology transfer, told a Senate subcommittee in May 1982, "The program that I started with and one that is very important to us in the future is the very-high-speed integrated circuit program. The VHSIC program has very great prominence for our military systems because it will enable us to improve existing systems and develop new ones with far greater capability. The VHSIC product will be used in advance-signal processing application for weapons systems, electronic warfare, communications, radar, precisely guiding munitions. It will enable us to do these things at a lower cost, we think; it will be smaller in size with greater power than anything we currently possess. Obviously, the protection of this technology is of highest priority . . . . Our immediate task is to protect the technical data, the military hardware that is now being developed, before it is too late to prevent the dissemination of these technologies to our adversaries."[15]

The issue of control of very-high-speed integrated circuits technology was one in which I saw Bryen's work at the Pentagon dovetailing with Israel's needs. As time passed, the more deeply I examined the Defense Department's technology transfer program, the more obvious Bryen's sensitivity to Israel's needs became.

The JINSA newsletter served those needs in different ways. After the 1982 Israeli invasion of Lebanon, JINSA was compelled to defend Israeli militarism against growing criticism. The American television networks for the first time were giving Israel negative publicity by reporting on widespread destruction of communities, high civilian casualties and the relentless shelling of Beirut. The JINSA newsletter countered by citing "official Israeli reports" that the numbers of civilian casualties appearing in the press" are an extreme exaggeration." It reported that the numbers of civilians killed were small when compared to the thousands who had died in the Lebanese Civil War since 1975. It also sought to justify the actions of the Israeli forces by claiming they gave southern Lebanese communities like Sidon and Tyre advanced warnings of the invasion in the form of leaflets and opted for house-to-house fighting in those communities rather than the "easier" bombing method in order to spare civilian lives.[16]

The article quoted Israeli General Ariel Sharon as saying, "Only when we reached the final stage, when it transpired that there was no other possibility, we used more massive artillery and air force sorties against civilian settlements. We did something that no army, no people in the world — be it the one pretending to be the most moral and civilized one — would have done."[17]

The JINSA newsletter also editorialized on the ramifications of the invasion for the free world. Entitled "Israel Did the Dirty Work," the piece said:

Even before the dust settles in Lebanon, the world should breathe more easily. Not only has Palestinian terrorism suffered a blow, but so has terrorism organized and promoted by myriad other groups. Many countries have been victimized, but none have been willing to take the painful and dangerous steps necessary to eliminate terrorists or the bases. Israel has done the dirty work for those countries, using its soldiers and its blood to destroy elements that made Lebanon the center of international terrorism. Those countries that will benefit have not admitted the service performed, let alone thanked Israel for shouldering their burden.

There are those who warn that destroying the terrorist infrastructure will cut "radical" terrorists loose from "moderate" ones, thereby increasing acts of violence around the world. Perhaps, but the absence of a safe haven in Lebanon and the cutoff of the world's center of illegal arms as well as major training bases should also increase the difficulty of carrying out such acts . . . .

The open secret of Soviet ideological and practical

support for international terrorism becomes clear and indisputable. President Reagan and others who have long stressed the Soviet role must find satisfaction in their vindication and further satisfaction in the setback the Soviets received in this respect.

In its determination to rid its own borders of violence countries that would have been subject to terrorism against their citizens this month or next, this year or next.

Perhaps, as in the case of the Osirak [Iraqi nuclear reactor], public protestation against Israel masks private relief. If not, it should.[18]

In October 1982, Shoshana Bryen led a team of JINSA members to Israel, where they enjoyed an Israeli Defense Force-escorted tour through Lebanon, the Golan Heights, the Jordan Valley and several Israeli defense industries. JINSA President Saul I. Stern said, "Our Israeli hosts were extremely responsive," and expressed sincere thanks to Defense Minister Ariel Sharon and "to our friends in the Israeli Embassy in Washington, D.C. for their invitation, their invaluable co-ordination and support, and for their faith in JINSA's mission." Mrs. Bryen reported that Lebanon was receiving foreign investment and rebuilding at an unprecedented rate and that Israeli damage to the area had been overblown by the media. "The city [of Sidon] was not destroyed, the citizenry not ravaged, the shops not empty. Words like 'blitzkrieg,' 'holo-caust,' 'genocide,' and 'carpet bombing' are widely misplaced in relation to the cities of Southern Lebanon."[19]

The JINSA newsletter praised the Israeli invasion of Lebanon and minimized reports of the damage done to Lebanon itself. It did not report, however, that even within Israel there was widespread criticism of the invasion. Instead, it served as a cheerleader for Ariel Sharon, the brains behind the bombs.

Moreover, the newsletter used the invasion to advance its basic philosophy. As JINSA Chief Stern said, "Our visit with IDF and government officials reconfirms and underscores one of the basic concepts for the funding and existence of JINSA. From our meetings . . . Israel's importance as our country's most reliable ally and strategic asset in the tumultous Middle East, Persian Gulf, Horn of Africa and the eastern end of the Mediterranean became increasingly apparent."[20]

Stern also said that Israel's role in Lebanon proved her worth as an outstanding fighting force, a vital democratic and westernized state and a highly technological country which was unparalleled in the region. According to his article in the JINSA newsletter, "These argue persuasively for the continuance and enhancement of the special relationship between Israel and the United States."[21]

JINSA never passed up an opportunity to portray the relationship between Israel and the United States as a special, familial one. Frank Hoeber, for example, wrote, "There is no nation, except perhaps England, with which the United States has closer historical and emotional ties than Israel . . . . But because history put Israel in the heart of the Middle East, these ties go far beyond the emotional — or personal, if you will. Of geopolitical necessity, the bonds are also strategic. This is often true of family members with common 'strategic interests' — how to utilize their resources of people and material to achieve their goals of survival, financial and societal position, etc. It is difficult to subordinate personal and policy differences (even animosities, clear or ambiguous) to a long view of their common interests, and at times it is apparently impossible to 'live with one another.' This may be in part because of the perception and resentment of the dependency of the younger, smaller and weaker party, even as among siblings or children and parents. Yet, as in the latter case, the mutual dependency, the need for each other, is much greater than commonly noted. If Israel cannot survive without U.S. economic, military and political support, the United States is also dependent on the only real, democratic, strategically-placed ally it has in the Middle East . . . .[22]

"Prime Minister Begin even used language consistent with our above analogy to the family by saying that the United States was treating Israel 'like a vassal state or a rebellious child.' But most families do survive, whether out of love or common need —if the two can be separated,"[23] concluded Hoeber.

Not only did JINSA depict Israel and the United States as part of the same family, but it also posited the idea that Israel was our only reliable ally in the world. Following the 1983 invasion of Grenada, an October 1983 JINSA editorial entitled "Alone Together," said,

> It is frustrating and disappointing to find ourselves standing virtually alone after having the courage to liberate Grenada. In the United Nations, we were supported only by those countries of the Caribbean who were threatened by Grenada; El Salvador; and Israel. Israel understood and approved because it has been in similar situations and has felt similar political isolation for its courage. In light of Grenada, and the lonely position to which the Administration exposed itself, we should reevaluate our previous hasty and ill-advised criticism of Israel for its preemptive bombing of the Iraqi nuclear reactor and for Operation Peace for Galilee for which it was similarly castigated.
>
> There is an uncanny similarity (although difference in scale) between the pictures of the stockpiled equipment the Israelis found in PLO tunnels, and the equipment found by the U.S. in Grenada . . . . The

American and Israeli governments may never see eye-to-eye on the details, but both have elected to pursue policies that do not wait for citizens to be held hostage or killed before acting. Both have limits beyond which phoney diplomacy will not be acceptable. Both understand the tangled web of Soviet involvement through surrogates in small countries and radical organizations.

There is a basis in this for coordination and cooperation between the U.S. and Israel to advance the national interests of both countries. Having demonstrated admirable clarity of purpose in Grenada, the U.S. should turn now to the Middle East and do the same, in concert with the only country of the region which shares our essential outlook — Israel. It is gratifying that, as we go to press signs point in that direction.[24]

JINSA had also succeeded in achieving an impressive circulation of its newsletter and articles beyond its members. It received its biggest boost from *Current News*, a Pentagon publication which compiles military-related articles and is sent to 15,000 government and military personnel daily, including the White House, the State Department, the National Security Agency and top echelon offices of the military establishment. The *New York Times* reported that *Current News* "asserts a considerable influence on national policy by providing a cross section of press coverage on a wide range of national security issues . . . . 'Our problem is one of selectivity,' a *Current News* editor told the *Times*. We can use less than 10 percent of the stories that make it through our screening process, so our choices are based on what we think are the most important stories and who covered them best'."[25]

In July 1983, JINSA expressed its gratitude to the Pentagon's *Current News* for including articles from the past 18 issues of its newsletter in its clips.[26] A simple count revealed that the first JINSA newsletter story used by *Current News* came from the May 1981 issue. May 1981, was the month that Stephen Bryen went to work for the Pentagon.

CHAPTER 9

WHAT PRICE ISRAEL?

The Reagan years were good to Stephen and Shoshana Bryen, Richard Perle and Leslie Barr. Their career goals were being reached and they were earning good money. They also had power. Increasingly, Richard Perle and Stephen Bryen were quoted in the newspapers and appeared on television news shows. Their dreams seemed to be coming true — and it was all in the family!

Israel, on the other hand, was encountering severe economic problems. Defense expenditures had outpaced revenues several years earlier, and inflation was between 200 and 300 percent.* Israelis could walk into banks and bounce checks without having the teller bat an eye.[1] While some hoped that Israel's rapidly growing arms and communication industries would eventually lead the country out of its economic quagmire, there was little hope that the problems would be solved in the near future. Israel sorely needed a well-balanced economy. It could only sell so many oranges and cans of olive oil.

News about Israel's economic disaster seldom appeared in American newspapers. Furthermore, the U.S. press did not seem interested in exploring the expanding role of the U.S. Government in the Israeli economy. It was a sensitive issue for the Israelis — precisely the kind of dirty laundry they did not want aired outside of the family.

---

*On October 27, 1984, *The Washington Post* reported that the Israeli inflation rate had reached 1,000%.

The General Accounting Office, therefore, made big news on June 24, 1983, when it published a 75-page report on the state of Israel's economy. The GAO, a research arm of Congress, detailed for the first time the level and nature of U.S. military and economic aid to Israel, Israel's mushrooming foreign debt, its obvious inability to repay the debt and its consequent need for still more U.S. aid. It noted that Israel was the largest recipient of U.S. assistance and that Israel received aid on the most favorable of terms. The problem, said the GAO, is that Israel's military expenditures keep growing, as do its debts and economic problems. Therefore, not only will Israel need more U.S. money, but it will need it on still more favorable terms. According to the GAO, Israel also is likely to ask the United States to forgive some of the past loans.[2]

The Israelis tried to deflect criticism of high military spending levels and a floundering economy by using the report as an appeal for more grants and good public relations. The *New York Times* reported June 26 that, "Israeli embassy officials said they were very pleased with the report because it stressed Israel's problems in repaying its debts. The Israelis, and their supporters in Congress, have persistently argued for high levels of grants, arguing that Israel needs the assistance for its security and that it needs the grants because otherwise it might not be able to meet its debts."[3]

In reality, the GAO report was a political "hot potato." In addition to the previously unreported economic and defense spending data, the report contained frank assessments by U.S. and Israeli military leaders of potential adversaries, as well as strategies for dealing with them. Career Pentagon officials interviewed for the report were often in sharp disagreement with their Israeli counterparts. In sum, the report revealed data and expressed opinions which did not reflect favorably on Israel. The main thrust of the GAO analysis depicted Israel as a spoiled child of the United States. Unable to control its excesses, it threw constant tantrums for a greater allowance. The GAO concluded that this situation threatened the U.S. economy, and that a lasting peace in the Middle East would be a much less expensive alternative to the spiraling arms race — and in fact represented the only real solution.

The GAO realized that the report was controversial and attempted to appease opponents by releasing to the public an "unclassified" version of the report which deleted "sensitive" information. Shortly thereafter, the American-Arab Anti-Discrimination Committee [ADC] acquired the uncensored version, published it in paperback and distributed it to the public.[4] This uncensored version of the report confirmed that the material deleted would indeed embarrass Israel but would not threaten national security interests.

The United States granted Israel approximately $1.4 billion in foreign military sales [FMS] credits, which came out of the U.S. Defense Department budget and enabled Israel to buy American-made weapons. Not only was Israel the largest recipient of such aid among nations, but it was given the money on the most favorable terms, including the right to receive grant funds, which do not have to be paid back, before loans, which do, and the right to defer interest payments for many years.[5]

One passage deleted from the declassified version read, "According to the Central Intelligence Agency, Israeli expectations are that the United States will fund half of its defense budget. Israeli documents show that U.S. assistance funded 37 percent of its defense budget for fiscal year 1982."[6]

The report also provided extensive, little known details on Israel's defense relationship with the United States. For instance, it reported that the Israeli military procurement mission in New York was responsible for more than $1.4 billion a year in purchases from the United States, which accounted for about 40 percent of Israel's annual military budget. The office made about 30,000 purchases a year, of which about 100 were for more than $1 million each, and 85 percent for less than $5,000 each.

In listing the special concessions provided Israel by the United States, the report noted that Israel was the first country to be exempted from repaying a portion of its military debt to the United States. In the aftermath of the 1973 Middle East war, Israel was "forgiven" the repayment of half of its military credits.

Israel was also granted 30-year repayment periods for its military loans, in contrast to the 12 years allowed most recipients. For the first 10 years, Israel pays only the interest on the loans. This is followed by 20 years of spread-out payments for interest and principal.

In addition to liberal repayment terms, Israel receives "cash flow financing," which means that since 1974 Israel has been able to use its military credits from the United States to pay the installments on military equipment ordered. According to the GAO, this contrasts with the more stringent requirements on most other countries.

Under the usual arrangements, the United States required that a buyer set aside the full cost of an item when the order is placed. Thus, if an order amounts to $100 million, military credits for that amount must be drawn down from the credit line, even though actual payments may be made years later. This was to insure that the purchasing country had enough money to pay for an order. Israel, however, was allowed to draw down only the amount needed for that year's payment. On the hypothetical $100 million order, Israel needed to draw down only $50 million for that year's payment and could use the other $50 million for something else.

In addition to these liberal repayment terms, a little-noted 1979 agreement gave Israel the opportunity to bid on Pentagon contracts, a privilege denied most other countries.

Despite these grants, loans and liberal terms, the Israelis continued to press the U.S. for more and more money and more extensive privileges. According to the GAO, "Israel wants the United States to: formally encourage major U.S. military equipment exporters to conclude buy-back arrangements with Israeli manufacturers; encourage DOD contractors to involve Israeli manufacturers as subcontractors; exercise a liberal policy with regard to reciprocal transfers of advance technologies; and assist in the modernization of Israeli industry. Further, Israel requests permission to provide maintenance and refurbishing services to U.S. forces stationed overseas." This latter request sounded very much like the proposal Bryen had advocated in the JINSA newsletter for improving "strategic cooperation" and establishing a U.S. presence in the Middle East. Although Israeli officials asserted that U.S. sales to the Arab states required even greater aid to Israel, a deleted passage of the GAO report quoted Defense Department officials as stating that they "generally believe current FMS levels are sufficient for Israel's needs."[7]

The "Economic Support Fund" [ESF] provided Israel with additional assistance. "The program, since 1981 [when Mr. Reagan took office], has been an all grant transfer of cash provided to support the Israeli economy and help the country address its balance of payments problems," reported the GAO.[8]

"Although U.S. assistance has been large and provided under liberal terms," the GAO explained, "U.S. decision makers are now faced with an increasing dilemma in continuing to bolster Israel's economy and ensure support of its budget. For the first time, beginning in fiscal year 1982, ESF disbursement to Israel was less than Israeli military debt repayments. This net flow of funds . . . will continue to grow in the 1980s and contribute to an overall increasing Israeli need for foreign currency. Consequently, it is likely that Israel will intensify its requests to the United States for increased amounts of ESF, forgiving and rescheduling current debt, better terms on future loans, and through U.S. assistance as consumers of Israeli products."[9]

The bottom line was that despite all the favorable treatment it received from the United States in the past decade, Israel was drowning in its own economic problems. The classified portions of the report forecast a crisis building as Israel found itself unable to repay its foreign debt of more than $20 billion in installments which were just beginning to peak. With the United States holding 45 percent of the total debt, Israel by 1993 would need $995 million in extra U.S. aid each year just to service its debt to American taxpayers![10]

The report's deleted passages described further the threat which Israel's problems pose for the U.S. "Even if the United States increased its economic assistance to maintain fiscal year 1982 purchasing power, substantial deficits would still result. In addition, since there is political linkage between aid to Israel and Egypt, the Congress would have to consider the double budgetary impact of such a step . . . . If the United States were to forgive more of the loans it would have a direct effect in increasing the U.S. budget."[11]

In sum, Israel's severe economic problems not only were worsening, but also were threatening to damage the financial well-being of the United States. Since there was little chance that Israel would come to peace with its Arab neighbors, the GAO's discussion of possible solutions centered on Israel's only major industry capable of bringing in foreign currency: arms exports.

"A large part of Israel's resources are devoted to building and maintaining its defense industry. Because of the relatively short production runs on major items of military equipment, Israel pursues an aggressive export program to help offset the large capital investments and high overhead involved in the production process," the GAO said.[12]

"Israel's world exports of military equipment reached $1.2 billion in 1981 (up from $400 million in 1977). Small arms, ammunition, communications and electronics, as well as obsolete military equipment constitute the bulk of the exports. Sales and major military equipment, however, account for an increasing portion of the total."[13]

Quoting from an unnamed 1982 U.S. report, the GAO explained how Israeli military aggression assisted its arms exports. "The demand for Israel's military equipment is growing. Israel's increased capabilities in the production of high-technology military items and the growing demand for this equipment will serve to boost foreign sales. The market for Israeli-produced equipment will be enhanced because its effectiveness in combat was demonstrated in Lebanon."[14]

The GAO concluded that Israel's only hope for a solution to its balance of payments deficit lay in substantially increasing its arms exports. The GAO also noted the consequences of this for the U.S. "It is recognized that Israel is not a significant competitor in the international arms market but it is rapidly increasing its sales; for example, to Latin America. However, if Israeli industry and trade are eventually expanded to a point where direct U.S. assistance can be greatly decreased, the Israeli competitor factor in the international arms market will also have increased."[15]

The strategy devised by the Reagan Administration to bolster Israel's economy was to make Israel's defense industries more competitive on the international market. Ironically, the plan called for increased reliance on the Pentagon. The 1981 Memorandum of Understanding [MOU] between Israel and the United States included an agreement that the Defense

Department would set aside $200 million for purchases of Israeli weapons. Although the MOU was suspended after Israel annexed the Golan Heights, the Defense Department set up a task force to study the feasibility of arms purchases from Israel. "The task force determined that the United States could not procure, on a competitive basis, enough Israeli military equipment to achieve the $200 million goal," the report concluded.[16]

This conclusion prompted the task force to recommend further actions, including American financing of the modernization of Israeli plants and equipment; improving Israeli marketing; facilitating transfers of technical data and commercial data packages; developing more liberal technology transfer guidelines for Israel, even though the current guidelines already allowed Israel extremely free access to U.S. technology. Moreover, it said, "the United States has permitted Israel to coproduce U.S. defense equipment at a higher level of technology than it has any other Foreign Military Sales credit recipient."[17]

The GAO underscored the importance to Israel of easy access to U.S. technology. "Israel's technological exports are heavily dependent on foreign components. Israeli officials estimate that during 1981-1982, most of the exports contained an import component of about 36 percent. In Israel's fastest growing industry, the electronics field, about 35 percent of the knowledge is acquired from the United States in licenses production or technology transfer. Almost every Israeli arms production effort includes a U.S. input."[18]

Technology increasingly was crucial to Israel since its efforts to acquire more foreign currency required it to move beyond small arms and ammunition exports. Israel needed to become a major exporter of the "big ticket" military items. In addition to U.S. technology, Israel needed more U.S. money to finance the plan. Accordingly, the Israelis persistently asked the Reagan Administration to authorize other countries to use U.S. Defense Department foreign military sales credits — American taxpayers' dollars — to purchase weapons from Israel. In other words, Israel asked the U.S. to give money to other countries so that they could spend it in Israel.

Israel's dependence on U.S. money and technology was best illustrated by the battles it fought to win Reagan Administration approval for construction of the Lavi jet fighter. Israel considered the project to be vital to its high technology industrial base and military independence. However, the project relied heavily on the United States. The Lavi contains an American-built engine, thus U.S. permission would be required for third-country sales. Furthermore, the Israeli's wanted an additional $200 million in U.S. Foreign Military Sales credits to finance the project.

In 1979, when the Israelis first proposed the Lavi, it did not generate much controversy in the Pentagon because Israel claimed the new jet would merely serve as a replacement for aging A-4 aircraft. When it was later revealed that Israel had changed the Lavi proposal in favor of a more ambitious one aimed at making the new jet a competitor to U.S.-built aircraft, the Research and Engineering Office of Under Secretary of Defense Richard DeLauer adamantly opposed the use of U.S. foreign military sales credits to finance the project. According to the GAO, officials in DeLauer's office "consider the Lavi program an unwise use of Israeli defense funds and recognize the domestic political and economic repercussions of aiding a foreign country's aircraft program."[19]

The GAO also cautioned that Israel's quest for U.S. aid and technology could threaten American economic and strategic interests. "The potential impact on the U.S. economy and employment situation, or even the U.S. ability to control the sales of advance weaponry technology, should be considered in providing the concessions requested by Israel .... The most important factor for U.S. decision makers to consider is the extent that the liberalized steps might be setting a costly precedent. Other FMS recipient countries will most likely ask for the same. If these are granted, it will compound the long-range impact on the United States."[20]

The GAO's observation, coupled with the opposition from DeLauer's office within the Pentagon, set off a furious campaign by the Israeli lobby to win U.S. support for the Lavi. The November 1983 JINSA newsletter ran an in-depth feature on the Lavi project. Contrary to the GAO report and many U.S. Defense Department and industry officials, JINSA asserted that the Lavi "poses no threat to any existing American aircraft," and added that it "appears to be the least costly method of solving the problem of enhancing Israel's security."[21]

"From the Israeli standpoint," JINSA continued, "Israel's security is closely linked to a strong economy, and the Israeli economy must rely on exports in the future to remain sound and repay U.S. loans as well as to provide a market for U.S. goods. Israel's aerospace industry is the country's largest single employer, and its health has a ripple effect on the rest of the economy."[22]

With concentrated lobby efforts, the Israelis soon got their way with the Reagan Administration regarding the Lavi. Meanwhile, Richard Perle and Stephen Bryen concentrated their energies on the Pentagon's new program to control the transfer of advanced technology.

CHAPTER 10

A FOX IN THE CHICKEN HOUSE

When Richard Perle and Stephen Bryen stepped into their positions at the Pentagon, the word went out that they would not have jurisdiction over Middle East issues. Instead, their primary responsibilities were to be East-West policy, NATO, nuclear and conventional arms and technology transfer. The GAO report, however, had made clear the importance of technology transfer policy to Israel.

As Perle and Bryen settled into their new offices, technology transfer policy clearly became a top priority. An amendment to the Export Administration Act, drawn up by Perle when he worked for Senator Henry Jackson, gave the Defense Department a major transfer policy role. The law was due to expire in 1983, and Perle was leading the Reagan Administration's crusade to amend the Act in order to grant the Pentagon an even larger role. The Administration's proposals would place even tighter controls on U.S. businesses exporting a wide variety of computer and electronics equipment. Consequently, the business lobby fought the proposals and convinced several Congressmen to counter with less restrictive rules that would promote exports.

In May 1982, Bryen testified before a Senate subcommittee on the need for intensified efforts to stop the flow of technology to the Soviet Union and Bloc countries. Bryen told the panel he had expanded his staff to handle the immense chore. In his testimony, Bryen indicated he had to work hard to stay abreast with the cutting edge of military technology so he could identify, as a policy matter, what goods must be prevented from falling into Soviet hands.[1] Moreover, Bryen asserted that the effort to stop the transfer of technology to the Soviet bloc required more Defense Department controls over what kinds of goods could be shipped even to our European allies. Yet Bryen never suggested placing restrictions on technology transfer to Israel.

In February 1983, Bryen's office issued a 26-page report summarizing its areas of focus in the ongoing battle to control the flow of technology.[2]

Bryen also wrote an article entitled "Strategic Technology and National Security" which was published in the May 1983 edition of the *Journal of Electronic Defense*. In the eight-page article, Bryen summarized many of the views on technology controls that he had put forth in his 1983 DOD report and 1982 testimony before the Senate.

> In order to get [the weapons] they needed, the Soviets organized an elaborate collection effort that included attempts to purchase Western technology under various guises for "civilian" use. They also mounted a massive intelligence operation to obtain what Western nations withheld from them for strategic reasons. The collection effort was augmented by a well-orchestrated disinformation campaign that continues to this day . . . .
>
> The Soviets are not amateurs in the business of technology theft. They have long experience in making use of technology acquired from elsewhere. At the end of World War II, they stripped German industry and moved thousands of scientists and engineers to the USSR to continue military programs. Today, with

more elaborate methods, they are cleaning the technology cupboards of the Western World. They are directly copying advanced weapons in the NATO arsenal, largely by gaining access to the industrial know-how and processes that make possible advanced Western defense systems.[3]

Bryen emphasized that it was not enough for the United States to try to block the Soviet technology theft program alone. All of Western Europe would have to be involved. The buzzword used most often in proposing solutions was "COCOM," which stood for Coordinating Committee for Multilateral Export Controls. COCOM is a Paris-based office created after World War II by the United States and West European nations to coordinate efforts to block the transfer of valuable military equipment to the Soviets.* Bryen said COCOM in the 1980s was not living up to its responsibilities.

COCOM's work program has moved from a relatively simple and straightforward exercise to one that, under the best conditions, is difficult to execute, requires considerable sophistication, consensus and some means of measuring success as well as failure.

It follows that, underpinning the COCOM process, there should be an understanding of the basic strategic objective of the program as well as a means of assuring that on a practical basis, the COCOM program supports in relatively clear ways the common strategy. Expressed another way, for COCOM to work (and for the national export control programs to operate properly), the program has to make sense to the public. Unfortunately, for a variety of reasons (including a strong desire to experiment with increasing

---

*Japan has since become a member of COCOM.

East-West trade), Western governments have failed to tell the COCOM story effectively.[4]

What Bryen seemed to be implying was that the United States and Europe in recent years had become too interested in the economic benefits of trade with the Soviet Union and not concerned enough about military security. Therefore, the COCOM program was not the tough, military-oriented organization that Bryen wanted it to be. He envisioned a COCOM that would have the last word in American and European export decisions.

Bryen also argued that COCOM must also have the expertise to monitor technology and technology flow. Rather than focusing on products, as it had in the past, Bryen said COCOM must concern itself with manufacturing know-how, the generic technology itself.

> Even more significant, COCOM has no regular way of availing itself of advice that ties proposed transfers of equipment or technology to the strategic criteria in which COCOM is supposed to apply — namely the potential contribution to the Soviet military effort. This is because COCOM has no direct access to a panel of military experts drawn from the participating nations. For this reason the United States has proposed that such a panel of military experts be created for COCOM and that it become a part of the regular organization in order to provide advice and guidance to the deliberations of the delegates.[5]

Although publicly Bryen tried to appear moderate and reasonable in his advocacy of increased Defense Department control over technology transfers, he and Perle both "played hardball" behind the scenes. They fought major political battles on several fronts to overcome those who opposed their efforts. Bryen's goal insofar as COCOM was concerned was the creation of a COCOM military board that would eventually run the organization. The West Europeans were aware of the plan and realized its potential for loss of trade. The COCOM military board which Bryen seemed to advocate would be a major obstacle to East-West commerce, an important part of the economy of Western Europe.

There was also opposition in the United States to the technology control policies advocated by Perle and Bryen. Within the Defense Department, Perle was locked in a turf struggle with Richard DeLauer, Under Secretary of Defense for Research and Engineering, whose office traditionally had been in charge of implementing the details of the Pentagon's technology transfer program. The struggle came to a head on December 13, 1983, when DeLauer, in a memo to Defense Secretary Caspar Weinberger, accused Perle and Bryen of circumventing Deputy Defense Secretary Paul Thayer in an attempt to acquire more power over technology transfers.[6]

In effect, DeLauer was objecting to a new policy, drawn up by Perle and Bryen. Known as "2040.xx," the policy would have given them authority over most technology control issues previously held by DeLauer's office. Perle had bypassed Thayer, the Pentagon's number two man, and had interceded directly with Secretary Weinberger to win adoption of the new policy. DeLauer charged that Perle misled Weinberger about the proposed policy change and about the responsibilities of DeLauer's office.[7]

DeLauer also accused Bryen of attempting a bureaucratic coup d'etat by creating a new export license office parallel to that already in place in DeLauer's shop. This office would enable Bryen to wrest control of technology transfer licenses when 2040.XX was adopted. Asserting that Bryen wanted nothing less than complete control over matters relating to the cutting edge of military technology, DeLauer assailed Bryen's office for allegedly:

— Dictating the technical parameters and departmental positions to be used in negotiating COCOM's multilateral export controls on computer hardware and software, radars, robotics and telecommunications switching. The recommendations of DeLauer's office were ignored, he charged, and "This has resulted in politicizing the COCOM technical discussions, has raised serious questions as to the technical credibility of representatives to the negotiations and has given an inconsistent and thus confusing message to both U.S. and allied industry."

— Using outside technical advisers to support policy views on switching, computers and microelectronics "even though technical advice had already been provided" by DeLauer's office.

— Dictating the release guidelines for very-high-speed Integrated Circuits [VHSIC], even though the VHSIC office of primary responsibility is under DeLauer. "VHSIC contractors have already expressed their concerns indicating their potential withdrawal from the program, and raising the prospect of a class action suit," DeLauer said.[8]

DeLauer also charged Bryen with committing a "serious misallocation of scarce resources" in setting up the new office.[9]

DeLauer, who was a former executive of TRW, a defense contractor, was more attuned to industry's opposition to overly restrictive Pentagon controls. Many of his objections to Perle and Bryen's policies were based on the fact that the desire for stronger controls must be balanced against the need to maintain a strong and healthy industrial base from which the Pentagon can draw.

Moreover, DeLauer had good reasons for objecting to Perle's efforts to go over Thayer's head by appealing directly to Weinberger. As the Pentagon's number two man, Thayer headed the powerful Defense Resources Board, which months earlier had affirmed the authority of DeLauer's office to implement technology transfer policy. It became obvious that Thayer did not like Perle and was not intimidated by him. He was a fighter pilot who could still take the Air Force's best jets out for a spin. Thayer was also a highly-respected corporate executive before coming to the Pentagon. In the summer of 1983, Thayer removed Perle from the Defense Resources Board — a direct slap in the face to one not accustomed to such treatment. The Board's decision to back DeLauer on technology transfer undoubtedly heightened tensions between the two.

Thayer, however, soon found himself in hot water. In the summer of 1983, the Securities and Exchange Commission began investigating allegations that as an executive with the LTV Corporation, a major defense contractor, Thayer passed inside information used later in stock transactions.

The SEC's investigation of Thayer gained momentum throughout the fall. By December, about the same time the Perle-DeLauer rift surfaced, the details of the SEC investigation increasingly were leaked to the press. Following a string of daily reports which criticized Thayer's actions, but lacked hard evidence that he had broken the law, Thayer resigned his Pentagon post and vowed to defend his innocence.

It was never revealed how the SEC became suspicious of him. Newspaper stories indicated that unknown persons presented potentially damaging information on Thayer to the SEC enforcement staff.

The result of the Pentagon's internal battle was a victory for Perle and Bryen, as they emerged with unprecedented control over the Defense Department's technology transfer program. In February 1984, Weinberger informed Congress that he had overridden DeLauer's objections and handed Perle and Bryen the authority they wanted.[10] The new policy directive approved by Weinberger gave Perle's policy shop jurisdiction over all technology transfer issues, including internal guidance, legislation, liaison with industry, and international representation, and over technology goods, services, munitions, strategic trade and COCOM. DeLauer's shop was downgraded to the role of technical advisor. The directive also specified that Perle "shall monitor compliance through the Deputy Assistant Secretary of Defense For International Economic, Trade and Security Policy," Stephen Bryen. In effect, the order made Bryen the new "Czar" in charge of technology control in the Pentagon's growing bureaucratic empire.

It also made him the contact with whom other agencies had to work when coordinating the U.S. Government's domestic and international policies.

Weinberger's report confirmed DeLauer's charges that Bryen had set up a Technology Security Center which created 40 new positions and was intended "to serve as the hub for day-to-day licensing activities [and] provide close coordination in individual cases as well as broader policy issues which may require more extensive review and coordination."[11] The report also indicated that Bryen had placed a high priority on automating all information connected with technology transfer cases. The new directive, therefore, enabled Bryen to seize control of the computer system known as "Foreign Disclosure and Technical Information System," or FORDTIS.

The report said that "progress has been made in improving FORDTIS," which serves as the electronic repository of data on strategic trade, munitions and foreign disclosure cases and contains some of the world's most sensitive data on the cutting edge of military technology. "Recent improvements include increases in the number of terminals, the types of cases which can be processed and the number of reference data bases being developed for the system."[12]

"The number of operational remote sites has increased

from 12 (32 terminals) to 19 (60 terminals) in the past year," the report continued. "The number of remote sites will increase through 1985 when 50 remote sites will be in operation."[13]

Moreover, Bryen succeeded in extending the computer network to other agencies and, most importantly, to COCOM offices in Paris. As the report noted,

> DOD was successful in 1983 in establishing a secure teletype communications link directly between the Pentagon and the offices of the U.S. Representative to the COCOM negotiations (U.S. embassy in Paris). In addition, DOD has also established a position for an operator to assist visiting DOD policy and technical representatives in the use of this equipment. This new communication channel will be a major factor in expediting the COCOM license review process . . . . Efforts are underway to upgrade the communications channel to a real time basis and to tie an online computer terminal into the FORDTIS system . . . Means have been worked out to allow all-electronic entry of foreign cases from COCOM headquarters in Paris. Within FORDTIS, we have implemented the capability for management to track and control a case from its initial receipt in DOD until it has been closed by the responsible agency. After closing, cases are stored in an electronic historical archive.[14]

The stated purpose of this highly sensitive, high-speed computer system was to cut down on processing delays about which the business community had complained. The actual effect was to put at Bryen's fingertips enormous amounts of data on top secret technology and on who was selling what to whom throughout the United States, Western Europe and Japan. Weinberger's decision to shift jurisdiction to Perle and

Bryen must have been the last straw for Richard DeLauer. In January of 1984, DeLauer publicly announced he would be leaving the Pentagon before the November elections.

Perle's struggle with DeLauer over technology transfer policy coincided with another turf battle pitting Perle and Bryen against William A. Root, director of the State Department's Office of East-West Trade. Root, a mild-mannered, 30-year veteran of government service, was supposed to be in charge of the U.S. delegation negotiating changes in technology control policies with other COCOM member nations. But on September 24, 1983, Root, citing efforts by Perle and Bryen to undercut the negotiations, resigned his position in protest.

"The arrogance of the U.S. Government is rapidly eroding the effectiveness of controls on the export of strategic equipment and technology. Those who proclaim the loudest the need to strengthen these controls are doing the most to weaken them," Root said in an "open letter to the President and to the Congress."[15]

The battle between Root and Bryen and Perle had been brewing for some time. An inter-agency task force consisting of the State, Commerce and Defense Departments was formulating the Reagan Administration's position for October 17, 1983, negotiations with COCOM on new controls on computer equipment that would replace outdated controls adopted in 1974. Root maintained that the United States needed to reach an agreement with the Europeans in order to obtain multilateral controls that would effectively block the flow of valuable computer technology to the Soviets. A policy which lacked consensus among all COCOM nations, Root said, was no policy at all.

Recent events supported Root's views. The Reagan Administration, at the urgings of Perle and other "hawks," earlier had tried to bar the sale to the Soviets of Western equipment for the Siberian oil pipeline without first reaching agreement with the Europeans on how to do it. The uncoordinated policy turned out to be a disaster. Caterpillar Tractor, an American company, was forced to give up a multi-million dollar project, which also cost hundreds of American jobs, while European firms benefited from the new business. The Soviets got their equipment, a U.S. company lost millions, and the rift between the United States and other NATO nations deepened. The experience showed that Perle's "get-tough" approach to the Soviets, when implemented unilaterally, was counter-productive or, at best, an exercise in futility.

But Perle and Bryen seemed determined to stick to over-restrictive controls, no matter how futile or unnecessary. When the American proposals for controlling computers were presented in the first round of COCOM negotiations, the Europeans responded positively. They even submitted additional constructive proposals which, according to some, would have made the controls more effective.

On September 14, however, the day before the deadline for the United States' final response, Perle and Bryen announced that the U.S. task force which the Reagan Administration had formed would not alter its proposals. They said that (1) COCOM was an inadequate forum to negotiate the important computer item; (2) the United States should not deviate from its pre-composite draft proposals at the upcoming October meeting and (3) the real negotiations should take place later in an unspecified forum at which a senior Defense Department official would represent the United States.

That was the last straw as far as Root was concerned. "The clear (though unstated) Defense objectives," he said, referring to Perle's and Bryen's objectives, "are to demonstrate that (a) COCOM as it is now constituted is ineffective and should be replaced by a military committee and (b) Defense should replace State as the agency responsible to conduct the negotiations."[16]

Root asserted that the State Department was and should remain the negotiating agency and that the Pentagon's role should be more limited. He called for abolition of the Perle-authored Jackson Amendment, Section 10(g) of the Export Administration Act. Designed to give the Defense Department greater control over the export of sensitive products when it disagrees with the Commerce Department, the section requires the President to report to Congress if he decides not to follow the Pentagon's recommendation.[17]

"U.S. arrogance stems directly from the kind of thinking which led to Section 10(g) of the Export Administration Act," Root charged in a direct attack on Perle's policies. "Although it does not literally apply to differences between State and Defense on COCOM negotiations, a spin-off effect has eliminated the kind of cooperation between those two Departments which is essential for such negotiations."[18]

"The President has never over-ruled Defense on an export control case and probably never will as long as Section 10(g) is on the books. The required report to the Congress would indicate that the Commander-in-Chief was not the master in his own house. Defense personnel know that their views have prevailed on several occasions when it was generally believed that the President held different views. Accordingly, they see no reason to listen to the views of other agencies or of other governments. They are no doubt sincere in believing that they are thereby protecting the nation's security. However, the end-result is a situation in which it is impossible to conduct negotiations with our allies. Effective controls depend on negotiations, because the United States is not a unique supplier of most strategic items. The issue is whether to have ineffective unilateral controls (the result of rigid adherence to U.S. proposals) or effective multilateral controls (which can be achieved through cooperative negotiations)," said Root.[19]

The day after Root's resignation, the *Washington Post* gave a straightforward description of his open letter and reported that Root "said the most 'vocal advocates' of unilateral controls are Defense Secretary Caspar W. Weinberger; Fred C. Ikle, undersecretary of defense for policy; Richard N. Perle, assistant secretary of defense for international security policy, and Stephen D. Bryen, a longtime Perle associate and a deputy assistant defense secretary."[20]

"In response," the *Post* reported, "Perle denied that the Defense Department opposed working with U.S. allies on coordinated controls and added that Root never threatened to resign 'during the decade in which there were tremendously damaging leakages of technology from the West to the East. While not holding Root responsible, Perle asserted 'this administration is trying to reverse the mistakes that had been made in the past'."[21]

The *New York Times'* story on the resignation depicted Root as an outright opponent of tougher export controls.[22] In a letter to the editor which the *Times* never published, Root challenged this description by reminding the *Times* he was resigning in protest over the lack of U.S. preparation to negotiate tougher multilateral controls.[23]

Root also reiterated his desire to see Section 10(g) of the Export Administration Act abolished, stating, in effect, that it gave the Pentagon unbalanced control. "Defense personnel, realizing that even the President's views are of little consequence, naturally pay little attention to the views of other agencies or of other governments."[24]

The bureaucratic battles fought by Perle and Bryen seem to confirm they would let nothing stop them in their quest for unchecked power over technology transfer policy. They were playing dominoes for very high stakes. First, they knocked down those within the Pentagon who shared or challenged their authority to oversee technology. Then they set their sights on the State Department, hoping, it seemed, to replace it as the U.S. negotiator with Europe even though diplomacy had been the State Department's job for 200 years. Root's comments suggested that the situation had grown to the point where not even the President would dare to oppose the Pentagon's decisions on export control.

Root's noisy departure did not silence Perle and Bryen. Not only did they refuse to budge from the no-compromise stand to which Root had objected so vehemently but they also took charge of the COCOM negotiations in the ensuing months.

On the home front, Perle and Bryen began moving against their next target: the Commerce Department. The Commerce Department was responsible for overseeing shipments to non-communist countries, which represented the lion's share of the export licensing done by the U.S. Government. The Pentagon, on the other hand, had the authority to get involved only with goods being exported to communist countries. Perle and Bryen were determined to gain greater control over exports by challenging the Commerce Department on their own ground. They argued vehemently that Commerce was not doing a careful enough job of ensuring that other western nations did not re-sell valuable technologies which they bought from U.S. companies.

Commerce officials realized that a new fight for bureaucratic power had begun. One unnamed Commerce official, in an apparent reference to Bryen, told the *Washington Post*, "There are some low-level people in the Department of Defense who would like to have the entire export control system moved over there."[25]

The Commerce Department recognized that the policies being advocated by Perle and Bryen would have an adverse affect on U.S. industry. Industry officials were already complaining about delays and a tremendous amount of paperwork. The involvement of an additional office would only exacerbate the problem. But bureaucratic difficulties were minor compared to the loss of trade — and thus jobs — the new severe restrictions would cause. In an internal review of the new DOD Directive that gave the Pentagon greater authority over exports, Commerce experts wrote, "While its stated object is to reflect 'DOD's increased emphasis on denying potential adversaries western technology which could contribute to their military potential, its consequences could be a drastic attenuation of all technology transfer, because of the negative tenor of the policy statements and the sizeable and springloaded bureaucracy set up to control the approval process."[26]

The analysis continued, "Throughout the Directive, the only consideration for judging technology is its potential effect on national security objectives. While this certainly is the principal consideration, there often are also valid economic, industrial and alliance considerations which are not mentioned."[27]

The Commerce Department, however, lost the battle against Perle and Bryen. On March 23, 1984, President Reagan signed a Memorandum of Understanding granting the Defense Department new authority to review export distribution licenses involving seven high technology categories to twelve non-communist countries considered to be a "high risk" in terms of reselling the technology to other countries.[28]

The Washington Post reported that "The President's decision could amount to an effective veto power for the Pentagon over sensitive exports . . . . Led by Assistant Secretary of Defense Richard N. Perle, the Pentagon has argued that the United States can effectively control the leak of high technology to the Soviet bloc only if it could play a larger role in the export review process." The article continued:

The seven areas on the semi-classified Commodities

Control List include semiconductor fabrication equipment, many different kinds of computers, laser technology and certain types of numerically controlled machine tools. These technologies, the Pentagon argues, serve a "dual use" — that is, in addition to their commercial application, they can be used for military purposes.

Defense insiders and export attorneys familiar with the licensing process report that Austria, India, Norway, Sweden and South Africa are among the 12 countries believed to be major diversion risks.

The Pentagon has been seeking the right to review high-technology export licenses for over a year, waging a sharp bureaucratic war against the Commerce Department, which has sought to retain control over high technology exports to free-world nations.[29]

Assuredly, Perle and Bryen were pleased with President Reagan's decision, but they wanted more than this limited control over exports to the free world. Congress was considering revising the Export Administration Act, which had expired in 1983. Perle and Bryen recognized an opportunity to extend their authority to include review of export of dual use technologies to all non-communist countries.

On January 9, 1984, the *New York Times* reported that Defense Secretary Weinberger ordered Perle to prepare legislation that would increase the Pentagon's authority. "Perle has assigned his assistant, Stephen Bryen, to devote his full time to drafting legislation and getting it through Congress this year," the *Times* reported.

The House took a dim view of the Pentagon's push for more control over high-tech exports. Representative Don Bonker, D-Wash., said that while the alleged threat to U.S. national security posed by leaks of high technology to the Soviet bloc was serious, an even more basic threat was being posed to our economic well-being by mushrooming trade deficits, which could exceed $120 billion in 1984. Congress, he said, must do its part to help U.S. firms compete toe-to-toe with other countries by providing proper incentives.[30] Accordingly, Bonker was able to get the House to approve Export Administration Act changes that would decrease the Pentagon's role and encourage exports whenever possible.

"Yet even as Congress is about to complete the revising of our export control program, the Reagan Administration has been writing its own script through administrative actions," Bonker said in a *Washington Post* article. He continued:

> In January, the Pentagon greatly expanded its guidelines and the departmental structure involved in the review of export licenses on technology items . . . . With the latest White House maneuvers, we now have an expanded Pentagon role, new interagency committees and an endless series of regulations and directives.
>
> With the exception of food and raw materials, the most sought after U.S. products abroad are high technology items. That is the future of trade, and it happens to be where we have a competitive edge. But that holds true only so long as we can compete on an equal basis. The administration's policies here, if not checked, will impede our export potential.
>
> For many high tech items, the United States is only one of a number of suppliers. Unilateral export controls will only curtail our nation's export opportunities while allowing other nations to carve out lucrative new markets.[31]

However, Bonker's counterpart in the Senate, Jake Garn, R- Utah, held an opposing view and convinced the Senate to enact legislation that would increase the Pentagon's powers to unprecedented levels. Garn also took his case to the public in a *Washington Post* article, arguing that stronger controls over technology transfers must be the highest priority. "It is crucial not only for ourselves but for our allies. In Europe, failure to preserve that advantage could mean the difference between deterring a Soviet annexation of West Berlin and the inability to stop a Soviet advance short of the English Channel. In the Middle East, where Israel's survival depends on the technological superiority of its American-made weapons and where the use of force is a daily occurrence, the cost would be equally catastrophic."[32]

The diametrically opposed House and Senate bills set up a classic confrontation, pitting the two bodies against each other, and Perle and Bryen against the influential business community. The differences were supposed to be negotiated in a House-Senate conference. But differences were so striking that a quick compromise seemed unlikely. In Senator Garn's words, "The House bill is so bad that I don't know if the House is willing to come as far as they're going to have to come in compromise to be able to reach an Export Administration Act bill this year."[33]

Bryen did all that he could to help Garn win the battle on Capitol Hill. He compiled a lengthy report on technology transfer and concluded that only the Garn bill could halt the flow of advanced technology to the Soviet bloc. The report was leaked to Columnist Jack Anderson, who ran a story on it as the House and Senate prepared to slug it out over their Export Administration bills.

Anderson wrote, "The most effective way to stanch the hemorrhage of vital technology to the Soviets would be to strengthen the Export Administration Act. Instead, the House has passed a poorly crafted bill, sponsored by Rep. Don Bonker (D-Wash.), that would seriously weaken U.S. export controls."[34]

Bryen's report listed 14 specific areas where U.S. technology was said to have helped the Soviets "to develop new generations of smart weapons, to dramatically improve their airlift capability, to make their nuclear weapons more accurate and to enhance their command and control with better computers and communications."[35]

The report also emphasized the need to strengthen COCOM, stating that there was not a single study which proved that our European and Japanese allies were effectively policing either their own exports or re-exports of U.S. goods. On the contrary Bryen concluded, "In view of the lax enforcement efforts by certain COCOM countries, the cases that are detected and investigated may represent only the tip of the iceberg."[36]

Bryen's report ignored William Root's assertion that the Europeans were willing to cooperate with the United States to stop the flow of technology to the Soviets. Instead, the report suggested that insofar as technology control was concerned the Europeans were unreliable allies who could not be counted on in the on-going struggle against the Soviet Union. Bryen seemed to hope that such tactics would pressure the House into approving the Garn bill, thereby augmenting his control over U.S. technology transfer policy.

CHAPTER 11

EXPORTS FROM BEHIND THE ZION CURTAIN

Stephen Bryen's preaching on the need to protect advanced U.S. technology created the impression that the Soviets were working around the clock in the United States and abroad to get a hold of the latest breakthroughs, and that money-hungry Europeans were not the least bit concerned about stopping them. However, as his own report suggested, this was only the tip of the iceberg.

U.S. technology was crucial to the Israelis as well. As the General Accounting Office pointed out, "Israel's technological exports are heavily dependent on foreign components. In Israel's fastest growing industry, the electronics field, about 35 percent of the knowledge is acquired from the United States in licenses production or technology transfer. Almost every Israeli arms production effort includes a U.S. input."[1]

Apparently, however, the Israelis had not always been able to get the U.S. technology they wanted through official channels. According to a top secret Central Intelligence Agency report, made public in 1979, the Israelis had also developed an elaborate network for collecting U.S. technology.

> The Israeli intelligence service depends heavily on the various Jewish communities and organizations abroad for recruiting agents and eliciting general information . . . . Israeli agents usually operate

discretely within Jewish communities and are under instructions to handle their missions with utmost tact to avoid embarrassment to Israel.

Israel's program for accelerating its technological, scientific and military development as rapidly as possible has been enhanced by exploiting scientific exchange programs. Mossad (the Israeli intelligence service) plays a key role in this endeavor. In addition to large-scale acquisition of published scientific papers and technical journals from all over the world through overt channels, the Israelis devote a considerable portion of their covert operations to obtaining scientific and technical intelligence. This has included attempts to penetrate certain classified defense projects in the United States and other Western nations.[2]

There was thus great irony in statements made by Perle and Bryen about the need for better controls over technology transfers. While Perle claimed the 1970s had been a "decade in which there were tremendously damaging leakages of technology from the West to the East," he failed to point out that the Israelis, like the Soviets, were conducting covert operations as well as overt operations to gain access to U.S. technological secrets.

In their incessant railings against the Soviets' covert efforts to acquire technology, Perle and Bryen clearly had the effect of diverting attention away from any operations the Israelis might have been carrying out. They also painted the technology transfer issue as one primarily concerned with the United States' national security.

The reality of the situation was quite different. Entire national economies were at stake. Both the European and American business communities stepped up their protests over the economic consequences implicit in the controls that

Perle and Bryen were advocating. Even before Congress sat down to complete work on the Export Administration Act, the United States stiffened its enforcement of existing controls. One British firm was unable to get a license to re-import even British-made spare parts from America. Another company, Marconi Avionics, found that equipment it had sent to the United States for repair had been impounded. The material was seized in the U.S. under a Customs Department program called "Operation Exodus." The program, which was funded in part by Bryen's office, resulted in the detainment of 7,500 shipments and the seizure of nearly 3,000 more worth over $175 million between 1981 and 1983. Paddy Ashdown, a Member of the British Parliament, responded to the thrust of the program by stating, "The Americans are in a position to do more damage to establishments than the unions could have ever done."[3]

The United States was also seeking tighter controls over the export of personal computers. British officials scoffed at this, noting that such computers could be bought at nearly any store and were often used by children. Richard Perle countered these objections by stating, "We're using them now for things like missile guidance. They're going to transform the battlefield in the immediate future. It's easy to say it's silly to ban the export of children's toy computers, but it isn't children who are using them in the Soviet Union — it's the military." While admitting that it would be impossible to stop a diplomat from carrying any product out of a country, Perle indicated he was worried about bulk deliveries that could turn them into standard issue items for Russian tank commanders.[4]

Paddy Ashdown also objected to the large number of new items which Perle and Bryen were trying to get COCOM to approve for strategic controls. "The list the Americans are trying to get through COCOM isn't based on national security — it amounts to a complete inventory of their military electronic warehouse — over 400,000 items. If we accepted it, it would be an act of technological suicide," he said.[5]

Perle and Bryen did not seem overly concerned with the possibility that their proposals might spell technological and economic disaster for COCOM nations. Key institutions in Great Britain, like those in many Western European countries, were 90 percent dependent on U.S. technology. These institutions, like many of the European industries that were dependent on U.S. technology or technical spare parts to keep their businesses afloat, could not afford to wait for U.S. bureaucrats to take their time approving export and import licenses before they could get the goods they needed. When they needed something, they needed it right away. That was the nature of doing business in a high-tech world. Foreign companies would have to drastically alter their relations with U.S. businesses if Perle and Bryen got their way.

Or, as Norman Tebbitt, British Secretary of State for Trade and Industry, put it, "While the U.S. Government continues to assert in practice as well as in principle the doctrine of extra-territoriality, it is increasingly difficult for industry or government here to ignore the disadvantages of reliance on U.S. technology and U.S. supplies which controls bring. It must make government and customers alike less secure in their dependence on British subsidiaries of U.S. parents; and it must strengthen the argument for a British capability under British control in strategic fields — or as a second best turning to another country with indigenous technology and without pretensions to extra-territorial jurisdiction."[6]

"Until these problems are resolved, the difficulties that occur will continue to weaken the links between our two countries. Not least would be the weakening of industrial links," Tebbitt said.[7]

Tebbit's statements represented a natural reaction to what

he viewed as the overly restrictive controls that the United States was instituting unilaterally. It made more sense, he indicated in a veiled warning to U.S. industry, for European countries to buy material from someone who had all the latest in U.S. technology but who did not insist on compliance with the cumbersome U.S. licensing procedures.

The only country that would fit such a description — ready access to U.S. technology and easy sales terms — was Israel. And, as the GAO report suggested, Israel needed to become a major exporter of high-tech products to obtain the foreign currency it needed to solve its tremendous debt problems.

There was reason to believe that this is the strategy that Bryen envisioned. Bryen was not at all swayed by the European warnings of damage to the traditional NATO alliance and Western Europe's economic well-being. In February, 1984, Bryen, who represented the United States at the COCOM meeting in Paris, heard officials from West Germany, France, Britain and Italy complain that the new U.S. restrictions had "just about closed off" the American high-technology market to European business.[8]

Bryen further aggravated the Europeans by announcing that unprecedented new U.S. controls would be put in effect that summer to control technology "which is carried in the heads of scientists, engineers and other experts."

Following this Orwellian announcement, Bryen, on February 14, 1984, Valentine's Day, flew from Paris to Jerusalem to open negotiations on a new bilateral pact designed to ease restrictions on trade between Israel and the United States. Bryen met directly with Gideon Patt, Israel's Minister of Industry and Trade, and began talks on the technological details of the planned U.S.-Israeli "Free Trade Treaty."

The likelihood that all of the policies to curb exports of U.S. technological exports would result in an unprecedented trade boon for Israel was becoming painfully obvious to American businessmen. According to *The Spotlight*, which continued to investigate the Bryen case after other media had dropped it, Israeli trade representatives were telling West European customers: "If the Americans cut you off from their high technology market, come to us. We can get if for you."[9]

A frustrated Northrop sales executive, who asked that his identity be protected, warned, "If the rest of the world is persuaded that it can gain entry to the U.S. technology market only through Israeli salesmen, who have the sole privileged access to our advanced designs and products, then Israel alone will control the lion's share of this trade which runs in the tens of billions of dollars."

The prospect that Israel would take over what traditionally had been exclusive American markets followed an emerging pattern. In 1977, for instance, President Carter, citing repeated human rights violations, cut off U.S. military aid to Guatemala. The Israelis moved in quickly and cornered the market. They also sent military and technical advisors to assist the Guatemalan dictatorship.

The United States, due to domestic political considerations, also restricted the sale of weapons and technology to South Africa. Again the Israelis became the main arms supplier of the Apartheid regime.

During the hostage crisis in Iran, the United States halted all shipments to the Khomeini government. The Israelis quietly continued trading with the Iranians, and provided spare parts and other materials that Iran previously had bought from America. When the Reagan Administration came into power in 1981, U.S. trade with Iran resumed. According to Commerce Department figures, U.S. exports to Iran in the first ten months of 1983 were $161 million, nearly twice as much as the $87 million recorded in the same period in 1982. But several times that amount of U.S. goods were believed to end up in Iran through indirect trade involving "other countries."[10]

As the war between Iran and Iraq raged into 1984, the Pentagon seriously considered abandoning its neutral stance in favor of Iraq. It developed a plan to restrict exports to Iran, requiring special export licenses which would be granted sparingly. The earlier battles between Perle and DeLauer over controlling the licensing process indicated that Bryen's office would be in charge of the licensing.

In a May 13, 1984, interview with the *Washington Post*, Iraqi President Saddam Hussein said, "Our information indicates that America lately did actually stop providing Iran with weapons and spare parts, and for this we are pleased. But her allies continue to provide Iran with arms." Hussein named Israel as Iran's leading supplier of U.S. arms and spare parts. "A top Israeli official, however, denied that Israel is currently aiding Iran, although he acknowledged that such had been the case in the past," the *Post* reported.

An official of an American aircraft industry, however, said, "Reliable sources have told us that the Israelis are still selling our products to the Iranians."[11]

Meanwhile, reports surfaced that in Latin America Israel was doing all that it could to encourage sales of its arms and to block purchases of American products. Representative Lynn Martin, R-Ill., upon returning from a tour of South America, charged that Israeli arms merchants were bribing Ecuadorian Government officials to buy American-made fighter jets from them instead of from the U.S. firms.

"There's no question in anybody's mind that money passed under the table," Martin said. She added that the U.S. should warn Israel and other countries that engage in such practices that we no longer will tolerate such transactions. Martin recommended that U.S. aid to Israel should include a proviso barring it from trying to obstruct direct American imports.[12]

So the Israelis, in the spirit of international trade scavengers, had a history of circling over U.S. trouble spots and then moving in to control former U.S. markets. The new Israeli strategy was much more grandiose, aiming to slide into the lucrative electronics and high-tech trade in Western Europe. Israel's economic survival appeared to hinge on the strategy. Their economic recovery plan had no chance of working if the United States continued to dominate the European market.

The Israeli Government could not afford to worry about such issues as technology transfer. On the contrary, it was doing all that it could to encourage exports — particularly in the high-tech area. In the early 1980s, Israel negotiated a free-trade pact with the European Economic Community. In 1983 the British-Israeli Chamber of Commerce reported that exports to Britain had reached record levels. According to the *Jerusalem Post*, Martin Mendoza, chairman of the British-Israeli Chamber, said that "more British companies were beginning to appreciate the advantages of working through Israel on joint ventures, particularly if they wanted to sell to America. They also were increasingly aware of Israel's high standards in technology."[13]

Gideon Patt, Israel's Minister of Trade and Industry, reported that the government has "initiated and encouraged the establishment of a network of institutions and bodies, each dealing with a specific facet of export promotion including the provision of various types of assistance to importers interested in developing or expanding their trade with Israel."[14] These pro-export offices included the Foreign Trade Division, the Israel Export Institute, Manufacturers' Association of Israel and the World Trade Center Israel.

In the summer of 1983, Elmer L. Winter, Chairman of the Committee for Economic Growth of Israel, unveiled a new plan to enable Israel to become economically independent of the United States. Not surprisingly, the plan called for dramatic increases in Israeli exports of high technoloy products. The key to the plan, he said, was getting American corporations to open offices and joint ventures in Israel.

"Winter believes that many Israelis presently living and working in high technology companies in the U.S. can be coaxed to return to Israel to develop industries in cooperation with Israeli companies," reported *Israel Economist*.[15] Winter called for agreements with the United States that would require increased U.S. purchases of Israeli arms, refinancing of Israel's obligations to the United States, development of maintenance units in Israel to service U.S. military equipment, and development of a free-trade agreement with the United States. He also advocated the creation of a new high-tech research center, specializing in microelectronics, robotics and laser technology, that could help attract U.S. companies.

By 1984, it appeared the Israeli Government was following Winter's advice. The government scheduled a May conference in Jerusalem to promote joint ventures between American and Israeli companies in weapons technology production. Yaakov Meridor, Israeli Minister of Economic Affairs, traveled to New York and Washington to appeal to U.S. firms to join the conference and consider opening subsidiaries in Israel. "We believe we can show the world our potential technological ability, which has been dramatically proven in the last wars in Lebanon and can be applied in civilian industry," said Uri Oren, a spokesman for the Israeli Economic Office in New York.[16]

As the Israelis prepared for the high-tech conference, Perle and Bryen coincidentally were getting ready to explain the Pentagon's technology transfer program to Congress. On April 11, Perle told the Senate Permanent Subcommittee on Investigations of the need to not only improve security controls over U.S. exports to the Soviets and Bloc countries, but also to West European nations and Japan. He also advocated tightening controls through COCOM.[17]

To make his point that ordinary civilian technology could have important military purposes, Perle put on display at the Senate hearing an Apple computer that was fitted with special software and used by NATO battlefield commanders to select missile targets. Conceding that the Pentagon had not yet succeeded in convincing COCOM nations to agree to control export of personal computers, Perle argued, "Just as the increasing commercial utility of computers and their related technologies has made negotiation of multilateral control more difficult, so too has their increasing battlefield utility made it absolutely imperative that new computer controls be established."[18]

Perle continued his argument for computer controls by listing other advanced uses. "Other computer applications include: high speed burst communications; automatic status updates for the battlefield commander on the availability of weapons, ammunition, supplies and personnel; and management of maneuver control, fire support, intelligence/electronic warfare and air defense artillery."[19]

Perle also testified that, "Defense has become alarmed that Western commercial communications switching technology has permitted the Soviet Union and its allies to improve significantly their command, control and communications systems. Despite earlier skepticism on the part of our allies, there is now a generally shared concern that existing COCOM restrictions on communication switching are insufficient to preclude export of militarily-significant communications equipment and technology to the Eastern Bloc."[20]

Perle downplayed the growing opposition from U.S. businesses to his export control policies. He described a special project devised by Bryen to convince American industry to agree to tighter controls. "In 1984, we will begin a more systematic program of presenting the technology transfer story to industry representatives at both the Chief Executive

Officer and lower management levels. . . . We want to make our approach more comprehensive to all segments of U.S. industry, not just to industries directly involved in militarily-critical technologies. This is being planned with the concept that suppliers, middlemen and exporters also form a vital part of the voluntary compliance export control network."[21]

At the Jerusalem conference a month later, Israeli business-men emphasized the growth of exports of specialized high technology, the kind of technology Perle and Bryen wanted to control in the U.S., Western Europe and Japan.[22] One ardent supporter of the Jerusalem conference, the Electronic Corpo-ration of Israel [ECI], concentrated on production of advanced military communications and switching systems. ECI appeared to operate without the restrictions Perle and Bryen wanted to impose on other advanced nations. "The company is highly export-oriented and 75 percent of 1983's sales were to countries outside of Israel. Efforts are being made to strengthen sales worldwide, especially to the United States and Western Europe. . . . Sales efforts outside Israel are augmented by a network of agents and representatives located in 35 countries."[23]

Another active conference participant was Elron Electronic Industries. Elron's largest subsidiary was Elbit Computers Ltd., whose president, Benjamin Peled, was the commander of the Israeli Air Force from 1973-1977. Elbit also specialized in production of computers for military use, its primary products being avionic systems for weapons delivery and navigation, tank fire control systems, command, control and communi-cation systems for air, ground and naval forces, electronic intelligence systems and multi-purpose antenna systems. "Established in 1966, Elbit designs, develops, produces, installs and maintains a product range widely acknowledged as being in the forefront of modern technology," the *Jerusalem Post* said. "Over the years, Elbit has established a close working relationship with the Israel Defense Forces, to which it is a major vendor. Elbit also supplies armed forces in different parts of the world."[24]

The importance to Elbit of export markets was underscored by the fact that it opened offices in the United States, England, West Germany, France, Switzerland, Singapore and Brazil. The company's annual report for 1982/1983 said that its highly praised "Weapons Delivery and Navigation Systems" were being used in most Israeli fighter aircraft, including the Skyhawk A-4, Phantom F-4 and Kfir C-2. It mentioned that the company was developing the "mission computer, display system and stores management system" for Israel's newest fighter, the Lavi. The annual report also announced that "The major marketing efforts in Avionic Systems are now directed towards the export market. These efforts include adaptation of the WDNS in various configurations for retrofit programs that extend the life of combat and attack aircraft."

Similarly, the annual report said, "Elbit Ground Weapon Control Systems [used in tanks] have high export potential, which has materialized in substantial export contracts. These are expected to expand in the years ahead because of proven high performance and cost advantage over competitive systems abroad."

Elron Electronic Industries also held an interest in a company called Worldtech Israel Ltd., which was apparently developed in 1983. According to a *Jerusalem Post* article, the firm "prepares technology transfer packages for non-Israeli clients, identifies new business opportunities and released prospects in advanced technology areas."[25]

"This is going to be the best year in our history," predicted Uzia Galil, Elron president, at the Jerusalem conference.[26]

But the greatest market for Israeli military technology was the U.S. Defense Department. Tadiran was one of the largest Israeli communications firms and was half-owned by General

Telephone and Electric. A July 1983 article in *Monitin*, an Israeli publication, reported that one of Bryen's old friends had become involved in the effort to increase Tadiran sales to the Pentagon.

Recent information we received says that [Tadiran] employs professionals abroad who operate side by side with [arms sales] agents. Zvi Rafiah,* a commentator on American issues, who used to work for the Foreign Office, has been mentioned in this connection.

Rafiah: "I am not a lobbyist and am not employed by any Israeli government office. I am a private advisor to Israeli industries on matters concerning the U.S.A., and I help industries export their products to the U.S.A. I am not a dealer and I enjoy my job as advisor. In spite of the fact that American industry regards Israeli industry as a serious competitor, I can help Israeli products get into the American market, and this is encouraging.

In 1982, Tadiran locked horns with an American company, E- Systems, over a $39 million contract to produce two-way radios used in U.S. Army tanks and armored personnel carriers. E-Systems had supplied the radios to the Army for 13 years, while Tadiran had been a subcontractor to E-Systems. However, in 1982, Tadiran underbid the American firm and, consequently, the Army initially decided to buy from Tadiran.[27]

E-Systems protested vehemently to DOD Secretary Weinberger. Citing testimony of Fred Ikle, DOD Undersecretary and Perle's immediate boss, E-Systems pointed out that it was Pentagon policy to choose American suppliers over foreigners. E-Systems President John W. Dixon protested that his

---

*Zvi Rafiah was the Counselor at the Israeli Embassy whose relationship with Stephen Bryen was a subject of the FBI investigation of Bryen.

company was not allowed to bid on radios to be installed in tanks furnished by the United States to Israel. "Tadiran got the job sole source," he said. Dixon warned Weinberger that if E-Systems lost the dispute it would be forced to cease production of the radios, lay off nearly 500 employees, and make the Defense Department dependent on a foreign supplier.[28]

"Dixon also suggested that U.S. taxpayers are subsidizing the Israeli company since the United States gives Israel several billion dollars in military aid per year and that some of the money finds its way into Tadiran's coffers."[29]

Despite Dixon's protest, and the fact that he was supported by Congressional delegations from Indiana and Florida, as well as by Majority Whip Jim Wright, D-Tex., the Pentagon ignored Ikle's professed "buy American" policy and awarded the contract to Tadiran. E-Systems subsequently closed down the factories producing the radios and laid off several hundred employees.

Although strides were being made in expanding exports, Israel continued to have severe economic problems and was a long way from becoming financially independent of the United States. The Commerce Department reported that in 1982, Israel's exports declined slightly and its balance-of-trade deficit grew. Hardest hit were the diamond and citrus industries, making it all the more imperative that Israel's high-tech industries pick up the slack.[30]

While companies like Elbit and Tadiran appeared to enjoy success in the export market, the Israeli computer software industry, according to the *Jerusalem Post*, was "not living up to its high expectations."[31]

"Last year [1983] its export only came to about $15 million, a fraction of what earlier, optimistic predictions had been," the *Jerusalem Post* reported.[32]

While Israel sought to increase its export of computer

software, on May 6, 1984, the *Washington Post* reported, "The Reagan Administration may expand electronic surveillance activity to prevent sensitive computer software from being smuggled overseas through international telephone calls, according to U.S. officials."

The idea, which one Senate staffer called "another Richard Perle special,"[33] stemmed from a belief that computer software could have vital military applications, and that the software could be transmitted over phone lines. "Commerce Department officials and Pentagon analysts say they need a way to monitor the flow of international computer communications to detect illegal exports," the *Post* reported. "The effort to deal with potential software smuggling by wire reflects a major push by the Defense and Commerce Departments to place various kinds of intellectual property — especially computer software — on the lists of technologies that face export restrictions."[34]

In addition, the *Post* reported that COCOM also was considering whether to add certain kinds of software to its technology control lists.[35]

The prospect of a mammoth, U.S. Government-operated, computer surveillance system for the purpose of intercepting electronic communications carried implications of George Orwell's *1984*. The idea was completely contrary to traditional American values of privacy and constitutional limits on governmental search and seizure powers. Indeed, it seemed that Perle's ostensible objective of stiffening controls against the Soviet Union was destined to transform the United States into a mirror reflection of Soviet methods of operations. It was also clear that such a surveillance system would further hamper U.S. high-tech companies and harm their competitive position. In fact, by 1984, it was evident that the Perle-Bryen export controls already in place were hurting American businesses. In a March 1984 cable, State Department officials in the Far East revealed that Cable and Wireless Systems [CWS], a major Asian telecommunications company, was ending its "traditional reliance" on American equipment in favor of "equivalent and more readily available" Japanese and European products because of U.S. export controls.[36]

Quoting from the State Department cable and other interviews, the *Washington Post* reported,

> Officials of CWS say licensing delays have become "progressively worse" over the past year or two and have reduced U.S. companies to "unreliable, last-resort suppliers."
>
> This could mean the "near-term" loss of tens of millions of dollars of U.S. sales to the booming telecommunications markets of Hong Kong and China. . . . "A CWS policy of nonselection of American products was implemented two weeks ago," the diplomats reported.
>
> As a result, no American products will be included in a $25 million government project in Singapore, they continued. "Two years ago, they would have made up the bulk of the CWS package."
>
> "Cox states that U.S. products constitute an 'unacceptable risk' — especially in Singapore where the government imposes stiff, $25,000-a-day penalties for delays," the cable said, referring to CWS General Manager Chris Cox . . .
>
> He was quoted as saying that CWS puchases of American products had dropped by 28 percent from 1982 to 1983 and likely would be reduced by more than 80 percent this year. In 1982, CWS purchased 45 percent of its equipment from U.S. firms. The figure was down 23 percent last year.
>
> CWS is the system subsidiary of Cables and Wireless

Ltd of Britain, the dominant operator of Hong Kong's domestic and international telecommunications network and a major player in the development of communcations facilities in South China.

In 1982, Hong Kong imported $817 million worth of telecommunications equipment and $457 million worth of data-processing equipment.

"Two years ago, we were dealing primarily with U.S. products. . . . But due to a series of embarrassments caused by delays and confusion in export licensing, we have moved away from U.S. products and by next year we may not be taking any U.S. equipment at all," Cox told the diplomats.

The State Department cable provides some of the richest details ever made public to back the contentions of American companies that strict U.S. export controls cost them sales in the expanding international market for sophisticated telecommunications equipment.

The issue assumes added political urgency as the United States' merchandise trade deficit grows. It hit a record $69.4 billion last year and is expected to exceed $100 billion in 1984. . . Cox stated that Japanese companies "'quite happily' sell standard products. . . with no delay or red tape associated with license procedures."

He added that "most Hong Kong distributors would share the view that the delays, uncertainty and onerous paperwork would make it 'totally impossible to do business with the U.S.' and (they) would quickly find alternative European and Japanese suppliers."

"Once people turn away and find out there are other suppliers, they're not going to turn back," he said.

The diplomats said that Cox and his associates from

CWS — Glenn Smith and Samuel Cheng — provided specific instances in which American red tape had cost them business. . .

In one case, Cox said, the first phase of a $200 million regional communications network being developed for the Bank of America's Asian branches is being held up because of license delays for U.S. made components that need to be sent to Hong Kong for testing before being installed in banking centers of Asia.

As a result, the Italian equivalent will be used in the second phase of the product, Cox was quoted as saying. Moreover, he told the diplomats that products made in American factories of Emerson Electric Co. —which once held the largest share of the regional market — will be dropped in favor of the same equipment made by Emerson's British subsidiary.

The made-in-Britain product is not subject to the same delays because of export control restrictions, Cox was quoted as saying.

In another instance, Cox told diplomats of delays ranging from six to nine months in delivery of American products needed in a project for the China Merchant Steam Navigation Co.[37]

The incident with CWS provided a case study in the effects of the technology control policies advocated by Perle and Bryen: huge losses of business for American firms and the consequent threat of a huge loss of American jobs. Of course, Perle and Bryen were pushing for agreements at COCOM that would pose similar delays for Western European and Japanese firms. If they succeeded in securing these agreements, one of the few countries left operating free of export restrictions would be Israel.

CHAPTER 12

ELIMINATING ALTERNATIVES

As Richard Perle and Stephen Bryen battled for Pentagon control over the export of technology, and as Israel expanded high-tech export industries, the situation in Lebanon steadily deteriorated. The U.S. Marines stationed in Beirut as part of the multinational peacekeeping force became targets of sniper fire from fanatic groups. The Marines were intended to be a stabilizing influence in Lebanon, but instead they were becoming caught up in the cross fire of renewed hostilities. I recalled the nervousness I felt when President Reagan first decided to send the Marines to the strife-torn region in August of 1982. I felt then that the United States had more to lose than to gain by a military presence in Lebanon. I could only hope that despite the growing signs of unrest, the ongoing talks between the Lebanese Government and the various factions would produce a settlement and hasten the Marines' departure without further American casualties.

My hopes were dashed on October 23, 1983, when a terrorist on a suicide mission drove a truck loaded with explosives into the Marines' housing compound — killing 241 men. It was reported to be the military's greatest loss of lives since the Vietnam War. The tragic event focused public attention on Lebanon and the United States military role there. Criticism of the Reagan Administration's policy in the Middle East was mounting. The White House felt compelled to do something.

The Israelis, meanwhile, feared the attack on the Marines would cause a public opinion backlash in the United States. The U.S. Marines were initially sent back to Beirut to facilitate the withdrawal of the Israeli Army following the Sabra and Shatilla massacres of September, 1982, and Israel's merciless shelling of the city. Now, while U.S. Marines were killed as they slept in the Beirut compound, the Israeli troops were stationed safely to the south. It was becoming clear that the U.S. presence was not achieving the goal of bringing peace to Lebanon. Israel, on the other hand, could move its troops to the relative safety of the south, let the multinational forces prevent Syrian control of Beirut, and, in general, benefit from the work of the multinational force.

Israeli officials moved quickly to stem the tide of adverse public reaction in the United States. They offered to provide emergency medical assistance to the Marines injured in the bomb blast and to transport special equipment to remove the rubble. U.S. military officials turned down the offer.

More importantly, Israeli leaders told the press that the bombing, which Tel Aviv alleged came at the hands of Syrian-backed terrorists, illustrated that the United States and Israel were fighting the same enemy — Syria. The event emphasized, they said, the need for strategic cooperation between Israel and the United States. As one "well-placed" Israeli told the *New York Times*, "Now there is much more sympathetic understanding between ourselves and the Americans, who seem to be going through the same mine field we've been going through."[1]

The Israelis were also quick to link their offer of medical assistance with larger strategic goals. They pointed out that emergency medical care had been a major component of Israel's concept of strategic cooperation with the United States. The *New York Times* story said:

The question of American-Israeli strategic operation
. . . goes far beyond Sunday's emergency, and far
beyond the issue of Lebanon . . . Israel has long
maintained that it is a "strategic asset" of the United
States, that it deserves the extensive American military and economic aid it receives partly because its
armed forces can bolster American policy in the
region. Rarely has an opportunity to prove the thesis
presented itself as dramatically as now in Lebanon.[2]

The Israelis were ready to convert an American tragedy to
their own advantage. A little more than a month after the
bombing, Israeli Prime Minister Yitzhak Shamir and Defense
Minister Moshe Arens arrived in Washington to map out
strategic cooperation with President Reagan. Two years
earlier, Reagan had suspended a memorandum of understanding calling for strategic cooperation after Israel annexed
the Golan Heights. However, with the election year approach-
ing, Reagan knew that his Middle East policy was in trouble
and that a major move was needed to demonstrate that the
President was in control of his foreign policy.

Shamir and Arens sensed this, and came to Washington
ready to push for as much as they could get. And they got a lot.
After two days of intense talks, Shamir and Arens came away
with an agreement that wedded the United States and Israel
more closely than any previous accord had done. Although
many of the details were to be worked out later, it was
apparent that the new agreement was in line with the plan
Stephen Bryen had advocated in the JINSA newsletter so
many years earlier. Some of the agenda items that were
announced publicly included requirements for prepositioning
of United States equipment in Israel, combined strategic
planning, joint military exercises, better sharing of intelligence
data and use of Israeli ports to service the U.S. Sixth Fleet.[3]

Reagan also agreed to some of Israel's specific requests for military hardware. He approved resumption of delivery of American-made cluster bomb artillery shells, which scatter grenade-like explosive charges over a wide area. Delivery of the shells had been suspended in July 1982, when it was determined that Israel had used them against civilian areas during the invasion of Lebanon. Reagan also acceded to Israeli pleas that some U.S. military aid money be diverted to help finance the new Israeli Lavi fighter aircraft.[4] The Israelis had sought the arrangement for years, but it drew stiff opposition from career Pentagon officials who objected to American funds being used to help develop a foreign-designed weapon which would compete with an American-made product.

Of course, the main item sought by the Israelis was money. Israel was scheduled to receive $1.7 billion in military loans for fiscal year 1984, only half of which was to be repaid. The Israelis wanted the entire sum to become an outright grant. As a compromise, the White House made it a grant of $1.4 billion, and said it understood that Israel would need more money in the future.[5]

Finally, the White House announced that the United States and Israel would set up a political-military committee to coordinate military planning, maneuvers and the stockpiling of American arms in Israel. On the economic front, it declared that the United States was willing to negotiate an accord on duty-free trade between the two countries — a decisive boost for Israeli exports.[6]

A week after this landmark agreement was announced, another first took place: U.S. Navy jets attacked Syrian-held positions in eastern Lebanon. The Syrian forces struck back with anti-aircraft fire and artillery shelling of the U.S. Marine positions in Beirut. By the end of the day, the United States had lost eight Marines and two Navy jets and a Navy pilot had been captured. Two Syrian solders were killed and several civilians were injured.

The significance of the day's events went beyond the tragic loss of life and human suffering. For the first time, the United States had directly and purposely attacked an Arab country. Syria previously had not been considered an enemy of the United States. It was most definitely an enemy of Israel. Now the United States had taken on the unenviable burden of fighting Israel's enemy for her. In other words, Israel's enemies had become America's enemies. Bryen's dream seemed to be coming true. The U.S. was tied more closely than ever to Israel's militaristic policies and its "ein breira," no alternative, philosophy.

In the following weeks, the United States escalated its attacks against Syrian forces in a desperate attempt to prop up the Lebanese Government of Amin Gemayel and to keep intact the new "partnership" President Reagan had worked out with Israel on May 17, 1983. Borrowing from Israeli strategy, U.S. forces tried a policy of "instant retaliation" against those who fired on Navy jets and the Marines. That policy, however, did not deter the various groups opposing the Gemayel Government. The fighting continued to escalate. And American casualties mounted. The cry in the U.S. for an end to our involvement in the madness grew louder and louder. Finally, President Reagan, aware that the U.S. presence in Lebanon could harm his re-election efforts, announced the withdrawal of the Marines. Yet even after the Marines departed, the battleship *New Jersey* shelled Syrian positions with its devastating 16-inch guns. This show of American military might, however, was for naught. The advances of opposition forces eventually prompted Gemayel to re-open negotiations with them. Negotiations caused Gemayel to immediately abrogate the May 17, 1983 Lebanese-Israeli accord which U.S. Secretary of State George P. Shultz had helped work out to facilitate the Israeli withdrawal from

Lebanon and the positioning of U.S. Marines in Beirut.

The situation had come full circle. After all of the U.S. air and artillery attacks, the loss of hundreds of American lives and thousands of civilian lives and the waste of millions of dollars, the United States and Israel found they could not control the future course of the Lebanese Government. What was worse was that the entire fiasco — particularly the new strategic cooperation between the United States and Israel — had served to further distance Arab countries from the United States. "Even Washington's closest friends in this part of the world, Jordan, Egypt, Saudi Arabia, the Sudan, Tunisia and Morocco, have been expressing their discontent over the enhanced 'strategic cooperation' between the United States and Israel," reported the *New York Times* on December 12, 1983. Egyptian President Hosni Mubarak was especially critical of U.S. policy.[7]

Arab criticism of the United States climaxed on March 14, 1984, when King Hussein of Jordan delivered a stinging attack on Reagan's Middle East policy. Stating that his efforts to establish a dialogue with Washington had failed and that he no longer would continue that approach, King Hussein charged the United States had lost all credibility as a broker for peace in the Middle East. "The whole situation is hopeless because it just appears more clearly than ever that the United States has foresaken its position as a superpower and as a moral defender of the world. It has forsaken its position as a nation that stands by its word and its commitments. It has chosen to disqualify itself as the sole force in the area that could help us all move towards a just and durable peace. The U.S. is not free to move except within the limits of what AIPAC (the American-Israel Public Affairs Committee), the Zionists and the State of Israel determine for it."[8]

"We see things in the following way: Israel is on our land. It is there by virtue of American military and economic aid that translates into aid for Israeli settlements. Israel is there by virtue of American moral and political aid to the point where the United States is succumbing to Israeli dictates,"[9] Hussein said.

"I am very concerned about the United States and its double standard everywhere. The saddest point for me is that I've always believed values and the courageous principles were an area that we shared. I now realize that principles mean nothing to the United States. Short-term issues, especially in an election year, prevail. This is the saddest thing that one can experience."[10]

Hussein gave up all hope of obtaining anti-aircraft weaponry from the United States. He hinted that Jordan would turn to the Soviet Union for the defensive weapons it needed.

U.S. policymakers were warned by their own experts that their "Israel-only" policies would lead to the kind of abrupt break with the United States that Hussein made. When the United States and Israel reached the new strategic cooperation agreement in November 1983, career U.S. military officials argued in secret memos that the spectacle of the Americans and Israelis in military lockstep would alarm moderate Arab states and jeopardize relations with them. They also contended that the United States and Israel had different goals. America was contending with the Soviet Union. Israel was fighting Syria.[11]

Officials in the Reagan Administration, however, ignored these warnings. They called the distinction between U.S. and Israeli goals "false," and asked, "What's the alternative? Let the Soviets and the radicals win?" They also downplayed the possibility of losing Hussein to the Soviets, asserting, "The moderate Arabs are anti-Israeli, but they fear Arab radicalism more . . . Lebanon and Jordan want the U.S. to protect them from Syria."[12] Somehow, anti-Soviet policies had become confused with pro-Israel policies, and one wondered just where the priorities lay.

The enthusiasm of the Defense Department bureaucrats, however, was not shared by many military chiefs. Not everyone believed that close strategic cooperation with Israel was necessarily a good idea. Protests were voiced calling for careful study of the implications and potential effects of the proposed accords.[13]

The first meeting between American and Israeli members of the Joint Political Military Group took place on January 24 and 25, 1984.[14] In the preceding weeks, Shoshana Bryen and JINSA operated at full force. As the Executive Director, Shoshana Bryen wrote to the Pentagon office responsible for working out the details of the American position for the January parley with the Israelis. Mrs. Bryen apparently suggested areas which the office should consider as it formed its position. Soon thereafter, an official from the office called her to discuss her recommendations. She invited the official to her house for more in-depth talks. The official accepted. When he arrived, he was greeted by Mrs. Bryen and found Stephen Bryen also present. For the next couple of hours possible areas of strategic cooperation between Israel and the United States were discussed.[15]

Stephen Bryen's trip to Jerusalem to negotiate "free trade" matters with the Israeli Industry Minister, Gideon Patt, contradicted earlier assurances that he would not be involved in Middle East issues. In fact, Bryen made another trip to Israel in May 1984. Bryen had spent years advocating Israeli interests on Capitol Hill. Later, he developed JINSA in order to remain a public champion of Zionist military needs. The 1981 assurances that Bryen would not be involved in Middle East issues had therefore been weak at the outset. How could one expect him to suddenly leave those interests behind after having reached a position in which he could pursue them so actively?

On the contrary, it seemed that Bryen's work in the Pentagon was in fact a realization of the course he had charted from his earlier days with Senator Clifford Case and JINSA. On the strategic front, Israel's expansion into the West Bank and Lebanon had gone unopposed by the Reagan Administration. Moreover, the concrete, military cooperation arrangements between Israel and the United States which Bryen had envisioned many years earlier had become a reality. As the bonds between Israel and the United States became more explicit, Arab states, previously friendly to the United States, became increasingly doubtful of U.S. integrity. They charged that our blind allegiance to Israel had caused us to forfeit our credibility.

Bryen's work on technology transfer issues, for instance, clearly illustrated his ability to adjust to Israel's more pressing needs in the economic hard times of the 1980s. Israel needed U.S. technology to manufacture "big ticket" weapons and other computer and electronic products for sale overseas in order to acquire foreign currency and stave off bankruptcy. But it needed more than that. In order to increase exports, Israel had to negate United States competition in the export markets, especially in Western Europe. The major policies Bryen was pushing hardest for in the Pentagon could have just that effect.

Furthermore, Bryen's desire to restrict export of U.S. technology abroad heightened tensions between the United States and its NATO allies. Like many of the moderate Arab countries, several Western European countries were beginning to wonder if the United States was truly a reliable ally. The growing gulf between America and its European allies also had the effect of making Israel appear as the United States' most dependable ally. Thus, 1984 became the year in which the U.S.-Zionist axis emerged stronger than ever.

CONCLUSION

A RACE
TO APOCALYPSE AND ARMAGEDDON

When the Soviet Union launched its military buildup more than a decade ago, Soviet leaders determined that masses of weapons alone would not be sufficient to offset the advantage enjoyed by the Western nations, particularly, the United States . . . . The underground Mafia-like operation of those who supply the Soviets can be put out of business.[1]

Stephen Bryen

I really resent being depicted as some sort of a dark mystic or some demonic power. [I have] no troops, no votes only a power of persuasion. All I can do is sit down and talk to someone.[2]

Richard Perle

The most prominent expression of this anxiety [in U.S.-Soviet relations] is found in the two words "arms race" and in the awesome piling of weapon upon weapon, an ever upward spiral without end, a race to the apocalypse.[3]

Richard Perle

You know, Bishop Saliba, there are a lot of ominous signs around us: earthquakes, the floods in Louisiana. . . . They are signs of the prophesies in the Bible and are warning of the comings of Armageddon.[4]

President Reagan

In 1967, French President Charles de Gaulle declared an embargo on arms sales to Israel. It was a move that came to have tremendous historical consequences. Initially, Zionists were shocked by de Gaulle's actions. Hindsight, however, shows that the French President actually did Israeli militarists a great service. The embargo cut the chord of dependence Israel had on French arms and forced Israel to develop its own arms industry. The seemingly tough French policy gave the state of Israel a boost toward further independence and development.

As Moshe Lichtman wrote in *Monitin,*

All those involved in the Israeli (arms) sales thank de Gaulle for the embargo he declared on Israel after 1967. . . . Up until 1967 Israel's arms sales were no more than a few percentages of its general export value. Today, a quarter of the Israeli industrial exports (not counting diamonds) consist of military exports. Israel is among the first ten countries leading in arms sales. de Gaulle's arms embargo took place during the great increase in military expenses that were accelerated by the Six-Day War. That was also the time when Israeli industries absorbed sophisticated modern technologies in the metal and electronic branches and the production expansion of an economical "boom."[5]

Lichtman described all of the weapons produced by the Israelis in 1983: jets, tanks, guns, bombs, ammunition, electronic command systems and missiles. He explained,

All this is for sale, for export. All the important Israeli financial bodies have a financial interest in this export, beginning with the big commercial banks (mainly Discount Bank) and the two big concerns Koor and Klal and ending with all the factories connected directly with military export . . . . A close examination of those who have an interest and control in them reveals such expansive ties, that one may well define the Israeli military industry as the economically largest and strongest complex in Israel. About a third of the Israeli manpower is connected with military industries, which know that arms production requires maintaining the highest production standards, similar to those of the Israeli or American armies.

The advantages of independent arms production and arms exports are obvious: income from sales, less political and economic dependence, employment. The main benefit, however, is to help lower the enormous defense budget. The arms exports make production for the army cheaper because larger quantities of weapons can be produced leading to economies (of scale). The arms industries developed on this basis and because of procedures that began with the Six-Day War. In 1967 industries began producing arms systems called "main particles," or "main system arms," such as aircrafts and tanks. At this stage export becomes essential for industry to produce efficiently. Before the massive expansion of arms exports, the large manufacturers were totally dependent on the Defense Ministry and its budget . . . . Now the manufacturers are less dependent on the defense budget and many of them prefer to invest their own resources than to rely on army financing for research and development . . . .

Mordechai Zipori, the ex-Deputy Minister of Defense, liked to talk about the military exports in terms of over a billion dollars, but the official data are less impressive, supporting the assumption that certain deals never appear in official records. In 1980, military exports reached $680 million, in 1981, $810 million, and in 1982, $820 million. It is interesting to note that 60% of the exports in metal and electronic products (including transportation) are military exports. Thus it is obvious that all industry and exports in Israel heavily lean on military products.[6]

As Lichtman points out, de Gaulle's now-famous arms embargo brought about a new kind of military independence for Israel. But the GAO report cited earlier points out the irony of this new independence. Military independence from France, coupled with a staggering defense budget, has given rise to an economic dependency on the United States. Israel may now be producing sophisticated weapons systems, but it cannot pay the production costs. Thus Israel depends on U.S. aid to finance its military extravagance. In order to be competitive in the arms exports market, moreover, Israel relies on American technology. Easy access to U.S. technology is therefore critical to Israel at this time.

The irony for U.S. policy does not end with Israeli dependency. Israel cannot forever depend on American money to finance its own largesse. Its blueprint for economic independence — indeed, survival — hinges on the export of high technology products and "big-ticket" weaponry. This plan for economic survival will not work, however, if Israel must compete with Japan, Western Europe and the United States for export markets. Israel needs a definite competitive advantage. It is in providing this advantage that Richard Perle and Stephen Bryen seem to play a vital role.

The stated purpose behind the policies advocated by Perle and Bryen is to counter the Soviet Union. In their furious pursuit of tighter controls over technology transfers, they have exploited fully President Reagan's well-known, anti-Soviet positions. Yet an extremely relevant historical analogy seems to be going ignored by many policymakers. Israel is now grateful to de Gaulle for the 1967 arms embargo because it forced acceleration of its high-tech weapons industry. Is it not possible, even likely, that efforts to block all advanced technology from the Soviet Union will force the Soviets away from "dependency" and propel Soviet high-tech development? A truly tough, anti-Soviet policy would encourage a controlled dependency rather than force technological independence.

The construction of the Soviet natural gas pipeline provides a good case in point. Richard Perle was a major force opposing the sale of western equipment to the Soviet Union for construction of the pipeline. He and his supporters convinced the President of their view and U.S. companies were forbidden to sell to the Soviets for pipeline construction. As a result, the Soviets developed the equipment and material to complete the job themselves.

Philip Geyelin of the *Washington Post* reported,

"The pipeline's construction was given the highest ("defense") priority," says Edward A. Hewett, a senior economist for the Brookings Institution, who was one of the few who warned that the sanctions would not work. A crash program called for a regular report to the Soviet Central Committee and made the pipeline's progress a matter of concern at the highest political level. Workers on the project were cheered along evey step of the way. Banners were hung at factory gates proclaiming, "This is our answer to Ronald Reagan.". . .

Boris Shcherbina, the [Soviet's oil and gas minister], called a press conference the other day to gloat: the entire 2,765-mile pipeline running under the Siberian permafrost and across hundreds of lakes and rivers to the Czechoslovakian border and Western Europe has been welded in place; pumping stations are in the process of being installed; for all practical purposes, the line will be open for business to Western European consumers on — perhaps even ahead of — the original schedule. And much of the equipment which was to have come from the West will now be Soviet-made....

There has never been any reason to believe this power play had any effect on Soviet policy in Poland. And now there is convincing evidence that it had just the opposite effect on the pipeline. What was supposed to be a demonstration of the Soviet Union's economic vulnerability has been turned into a demonstration of Soviet economic prowess ....

The Reagan Administration didn't just shoot itself in the foot with the pipeline sanctions. It also gave the Soviet Union a shot in the arm.[7]

The pipeline debacle forces one to take another look at the Perle-Bryen campaign to stop mass shipments of computers to the Soviet Union. If the campaign succeeds, will this prompt the Russians to accelerate development of their own computer industry? And if so, will that enable the Soviet Government to have greater control over the pace of distribution of personal computers and avoid the "de-stabilizing" effects of massive imports of the machines in a society that is famous for keeping tight reins on information and communications? There is reason to believe that, in terms of the Soviet Union and its technological development, the effect of the Perle-Bryen policies will be diametrically opposed to their stated purpose. Necessity may once again force the Russians to respond to Reagan as the Israelis responded to de Gaulle.

As for the United States' economic and technological development, if carried out, the Perle-Bryen policies could have devastating long-term consequences. As previously noted, prolonged delays in export licensing already have cost American companies millions of dollars in business. Losses could be in the billions before long, and U.S. employment opportunities stand to suffer. Several American business officials agree that their companies will lose incentives for research and development and innovative production if they are discouraged from maintaining their edge in export markets by restrictive U.S. Government policies. "If we can't sell it, there's no reason to make it," remarked one corporate official who summed up the views of many.[8]

Even more serious is the fact that Perle and Bryen advocate new controls that go beyond export licensing and strike at the heart of traditional freedom of western scientists to exchange ideas and information. Perle and Bryen want to impose unprecedented secrecy obligations on American scientists in order to keep new advances from reaching the Soviet Union.

The National Academy of Sciences, noting that "current proponents of stricter controls advocate a strategy of security through secrecy," argued that "security by accomplishment may have more to offer as a general national strategy."[9] As James V. Siena, a former Deputy Assistant Secretary of Defense, said in a *Washington Post* article,

> But even a narrow conception of security, which asks how we maintain as well as we can our scientific advantage in competing with the Russians, "security by accomplishment," which assumes that science will serve our security needs best if it continues to operate unfettered by government-imposed constraints, is

the only sound course.

There is no reason to believe that we are collectively smarter than the Russians, or that we possess some inherent capacity to do better science. The reasons for the lead we have where we have it over the Russians are rooted in our histories, cultures and systems. Our freedom of scientific interchange allows science to grow at a natural rate, with all who are interested having the chance to test and build. The Russian passion for secrecy and insistence on orthodoxy deprive many of the seeds of scientific advance which are planted there of the nurture that growth in unbounded fields can bring . . . .

Science is, now more than ever, an enterprise. To be sure, the lone genius still surprises us by taking leaps beyond what others think or know. But most of our gains and growth come from the attention devoted to a problem by many minds, some more able than others, but none as able as the collective whole.

As you reduce the number of minds allowed access to a strain of thought, you slow the progress of growth. Science also defies compartmentalization. Those who study the basic elements of matter and those who study the cosmos feed off each other. To channel knowledge to those with a "need to know" assumes a command of eternal relationships that no one possesses. Science knows no such boundaries.[10]

In seeking to place new controls on scientists and the exchange of ideas and information, Perle and Bryen were pushing policies which were bound to eventually stunt the advancement of U.S. technology itself. Ironically, it has been this very sort of control that has caused the Soviet Union to fall behind the U.S. in terms of high-tech development. So while the Soviets would have no alternative but to develop high-tech industries as quickly as possible, boundaries would be placed on science in the western world.

While there was increasing evidence that the Perle-Bryen technology transfer policies would have negative effects on scientific progress and the American economy, there was also little doubt that the foreign policies they favored, and which were being pursued by the Reagan Administration, had led to the worst deterioration of U.S.-Soviet relations in decades. Perle repeatedly opposed arms negotiation talks with the Soviets and advocated military build-ups and the creation of space weapons, known as the "Star Wars" plan. Tensions between the nuclear superpowers were at frightening levels.

As tensions mount, the newspaper headlines are carrying the word "Armageddon" more and more frequently. To many, the term represents the site of the biblical "last battle," the quintessential struggle between good and evil preceding the end of the world. Much of the association with the term is mystical, as reflected in the writings of the Book of Revelations. Many people are unaware that Armageddon is in fact a real place, associated by some scholars with the ancient town of Megiddo, slightly northwest of Jerusalem. The area has been the scene of significant military battles in the area — from before Christ to World War I.

Ronald Reagan is one of the most prominent figures to refer to Armageddon. In 1983, he called Thomas Dine, Executive Director of the American-Israel Public Affairs Committee [AIPAC], to thank him for helping to win the fight in Congress which temporarily kept the Marines in Lebanon. Reagan told Dine, "I've turned back to your ancient prophets in the Old Testament and the signs foretelling Armageddon, and I find myself wondering if we're the generation that is going to see that come about. I don't know if you have noted any of these prophesies lately, but believe me, they certainly describe the times were going through."[11]

On another occasion, Reagan responded to a question about the prophesy of Armageddon by stating, "I've talked with a few of my own people because quite a while ago theologians were telling me that never before has there been a time when so many prophesies were coming together. There have been times in the past when we thought the end of the world was coming but never anything like this!"[12]

It is a particularly ominous signal when the President of the United States speaks of the prophesy of Armageddon. Of all men, he is in a position to make decisions that could cause the fulfillment of the prophesy in our time. The fact that men like Stephen Bryen and Richard Perle are allowed to expand their power and policies adds fuel to the fire. The policies which Bryen had advocated in the JINSA newsletter were increasingly being applied in the Middle East. As Perle and Bryen worked their way into positions of influence in the Reagan Administration, U.S. foreign policy in the Middle East became more and more one-sided and the "tough stand" position towards both the Soviets and Western Europe resulted in a wider rift between the U.S. and her allies.

Bryen's basic premise was that Israel would serve as the United States' most reliable ally in the Middle East and would help deter aggressive acts by the Soviets. He regularly invoked the threat of Soviet aggression in the Middle East, but a glance at the facts reveals an entirely different threat. Israel has swallowed up the West Bank, the Golan Heights and southern Lebanon. It has driven all the way to Beirut and shelled the city day and night. Furthermore, Israel has blatantly disregarded U.S. policy in its quest for increased exports and more land. For example, Israel continues to set up new settlements on the West Bank and to sell arms to Iran to be used in the war with Iraq. Both moves are destabilizing in the region and are contrary to U.S. policy. Any other ally would be criticized harshly for such acts, yet Israel pays little attention to U.S. interests, or the goal of peace, and still demands U.S. aid and "cooperation." Through the influence of Perle, Bryen and other friends in the U.S. Administration and Congress, Israel has obtained a "strategic cooperation agreement" with the U.S. as well as unprecedented assistance with the Lavi fighter jet.

The result of these "Israel-first" moves has been a dramatic loss of credibility for the United States among Arab countries —especially those considered our friends, such as Jordan and Saudi Arabia. Just as fighting in the Persian Gulf between Iran and Iraq reached nerve-wracking levels, and the precious oil supplies seemed threatened, the United States found itself with little influence among the Gulf nations. The thrust of previous U.S. foreign policy had been to ensure maximum influence in the region in case of hostilities and a threat to the oil supply. More recent policies, which paid little attention to our friends in the Arab world, however, had severely tarnished our reputation and credibility.

This has proved to be a major setback for the United States. Israel, on the other hand, seems to be benefitting from the situation. It has consolidated its control of southern Lebanon and has prepared for possible future clashes with Syria. Israel knows it must expand, acquire more land, water and resources, and build a solid economic base. In addition, it realizes that it must export more and more weapons and high-tech gear in order to acquire foreign capital. Present plans call for Israel to become the leading arms merchant worldwide. While Perle and Bryen devise U.S. policies that restrict exports and even limit the exchange of scientific ideas, Israel follows a "take the money and run" export strategy. To a large degree, moreover, it is U.S. technology which Israel exports. So while American aid to Israel — in the form of money and technology —helps Israel compete with the U.S. for export markets, policies are being formulated in the U.S. itself which limit and even hamper U.S. exports into those same markets. How long can the U.S. handle this drain?

Perle and Bryen are likely to continue expanding their power and influence. Their staunchest opponent in the Pentagon, Paul Thayer, is now gone. William Root, who challenged them from the State Department, is also gone. Another Pentagon opponent, Richard DeLauer, has stated he intends to leave the Defense Department. Perle and Bryen have ambitiously developed their bureaucratic empire, wresting control of technology and munitions licensing, enlarging their staffs and successfully fighting other agencies for jurisdictional authority.

The fact that Perle and Bryen spend so much time talking about COCOM suggests that it might be their next target. It must be remembered that Perle, as a Senate staffer, helped draft the amendment to the Export Administration Act which created the authority which he and Bryen now enjoy in the Pentagon. It seems only logical that they will use their current positions to create future influential opportunities in COCOM. As noted earlier, Perle and Bryen have boasted about establishing a computer link between the Pentagon and COCOM. Thus, if they are able to establish themselves as COCOM's "expert military advisors," they would still enjoy ready access to classified U.S. information and, in addition, have easier access to sensitive data generated by Western European and Japanese militaries and industries. They would also be more removed from the media spotlight. A most effective arrangement for them would be to place Perle in COCOM's Paris office and Bryen in Perle's position as Assistant Secretary of Defense.

Perle and Bryen have also successfully established a network of allies within the Reagan Administration. As Jeff Gerth wrote in the *New York Times*, "Mr. Perle's influence in the

Reagan Administration far exceeds that normally held by an Assistant Secretary of Defense. In the transition, he was able to place associates in important national security positions and, in the Defense Department, he has played a major role in creating policies on arms control and trade with the Soviet Union."[13]*

In the near future, at least, the activities of Perle and Bryen will probably give a good indication of what Israel needs from the United States. In the 1970s, when American Presidents were willing to pursue more even-handed policies and at least carry out constructive dialogue with the Arab nations, Perle and Bryen worked hard to keep Congress on Israel's side. In the 1980s, when Israel's economic problems required that it export more arms, Perle and Bryen fought in the Defense Department for more controls over American exports and a firmer grip on European and Japanese exports through COCOM.

Despite their contacts and influence, Perle and Bryen will find a rough road ahead of them. Israel's economic problems most likely will worsen, and the U.S. will not be able to support a foreign economy forever. As Israel seeks to expand its strength through military prowess, its expansionism may take on a more economic character, giving rise to new forms of Israeli colonialism. A renewed clash with Syria in the near future seems inevitable given current Israeli policies. Would an Israeli-Syrian war draw their respective allied super-powers into a Middle East conflict? Will Israel become actively involved in the Iran-Iraq War in order to see Iraq, its "arch-

---

* A few of the officials that Perle had a role in promoting were Ken Adelman, now head of the Arms Control and Disarmament Agency, Noel C. Koch, an Assistant Secretary of Defense for International Security Affairs and William J. Schneider, Jr., Undersecretary for Security Assistance at the State Department.

enemy," defeated?

It is certainly in the best interests of the United States to contain the fighting in the Middle East, and the U.S. clearly does not want to see an Iranian victory in the present war. Yet despite the fact that Israel does not support these and other U.S. interests in the region, the policies devised, advocated and instituted by men such as Richard Perle, Stephen Bryen and their network of friends place no restraints on Israel. While restraints are placed on even our NATO allies with respect to technology transfer, Israel is allowed easy access to high technology. While the U.S. budget deficits reach frightening levels, aid to Israel increases year after year, and Israel is permitted to use that aid to develop products which will compete with American products, such as the Lavi fighter. While U.S. companies are subject to restraints that limit exports and thus result in the unemployment of American workers, Israel moves into the markets previously in the dominion of U.S. companies. As special envoys are sent to the Middle East to negotiate a meaningful and lasting peace, Israel bombs Beirut leaving hundreds of civilians wounded and homeless. Why are the limitations and restraints placed on other U.S. allies not placed on Israel? Israel is, after all, an independent nation. And why are men like Stephen Bryen, who has been suspected of giving a highly classified Pentagon document to agents of the Israeli Government, appointed to high-level positions in the Defense Department? Whom are such policies serving?

These policies are not only detrimental to the United States as a nation, but are also contrary to the interests of world peace. The Middle East is rife with tension, tension which is exacerbated by an unrestrained Israel. The elaborate network of relations between the countries of the Middle East has been shredding rapidly. An unrestrained Israel, supported and financed by the United States, could cause that network to dissolve completely. If that happens, both the United States and the Soviet Union will be drawn into the fray . . . And Armageddon is right in the neighborhood.

A PLAN OF ACTION

The people featured in this book have a plan for action. That plan is a threat to U.S. national security and world peace. To counter them, we must also have a plan. As a concerned American, please take the time to do the following:

(1) Write the President, your Senators and Congressmen, and ask them to read the Justice Department's file on the Stephen Bryen investigation. Tell them not to depend on an aide or a letter from a government agency for an opinion of the case. Insist that they read the parts which are deleted and unavailable to the general public.

(2) Ask them to send you their findings. If there is any doubt that the case should have been closed, or that Bryen should have received a security clearance allowing him to take his current job in the Pentagon, then urge them to demand that the Justice Department reopen the investigation, and urge them to hold special congressional hearings.

(3) Write me to report the results. I promise that I will pursue this case until justice — and American interests — are served.

Please do this today. We want our children to see tomorrow.

Michael P. Saba
P.O. BOX 53018
Washington, DC 20009

NOTES

Chapter 1

1. Affidavit of Michael P. Saba, filed with the Justice Department, March 13, 1978. (Herein referred to as the "Saba Affidavit.") See Appendix A.
2. Ibid., pgs. 4-5.
3. *Evening News*, Pasaic County, N.J., April 3, 1978.
4. Saba Affidavit, pg. 6.
5. Ibid., pg. 6.
6. Ibid., pg. 7.
7. Ibid., pg. 7.
8. Ibid., pg. 8.
9. Ibid., pg. 8.
10. Ibid., pg. 8.
11. Ibid., pg. 9.
12. Ibid., pg. 9.
13. *Houston Post*, April 2, 1978.
14. Ibid.
15. Ibid.
16. *Washington Post*, April 6, 1978.

Chapter 2

1. Norman Podhoretz, *Breaking Ranks: A Political Memoir*, (New York: Harper & Row Publishers, 1979), pg. 351.
2. Ibid., pgs. 351, 357.
3. Ibid., pg. 353.
4. *Washington Post*, June 26, 1977.
5. *New York Times*, November 13, 1978.
6. Ibid.
7. Ibid.
8. Seymour M. Hersch, *The Price of Power: Kissinger in the Nixon White House* (New York: Summit Books, 1983) pg. 322, and *The Atlantic Monthly*, May 1982.
9. Ibid.
10. *Facts on File World New Digest*, May 1, 1976.
11. *The Economist*, May 1, 1976.

Chapter 3

1. Evan Hendricks, *Former Secrets: Government Records Made Public Through The Freedom of Information Act*,

(Washington, D.C.: Campaign For Political Rights, 1982).

2. Letter of E. Ross Buckley, Chief of Freedom of Information/Privacy Unit, Criminal Division, U.S. Department of Justice, to J.R. AbiNader, Executive Director, National Association of Arab Americans, August 6, 1980.
3. *Jewish Institute for National Security Affairs (JINSA) Newsletter*, Volume II, Number 4.
4. *JINSA Newsletter*, April, 1980.
5. *JINSA Newsletter*, March, 1981.
6. Ibid.
7. *JINSA Newsletter*, February, 1981.
8. *JINSA Newsletter*, April, 1981.
9. *JINSA Newsletter*, March, 1981.
10. *JINSA Newsletter*, February, 1981.
11. Ibid.
12. Ibid.
13. Ibid.

Chapter 4

1. *JINSA Newsletter*, February 1981.
2. Ibid.
3. Ibid.
4. Ibid.
5. Letter of David J. Sadd, Executive Director of NAAA, to the Honorable Edward Zorinsky, Chairman of the House Armed Services Committee, July 17, 1981.
6. *Congressional Record*, July 16, 1981.
7. Ibid.
8. Ibid.
9. Ibid.
10. Ibid.
11. *Focus*, February 15, 1982.
12. Letter of Sadd to James McCue, Chief, Security Division, Office of the Secretary of Defense, Department of Defense, August 19, 1981.
13. Letter of McCue to Sadd, September 2, 1981.
14. Letter of William H. Taft, General Counsel, Department of Defense, to Sadd, September 28, 1981.
15. Letter to Fred C. Ikle, Under Secretary of Defense, Department of Defense, to Sadd, October 13, 1981.

Chapter 5

1. Memorandum of Attorney General William French Smith, May 4, 1981; and testimony of Jonathon C. Rose, Assistant Attorney General, before the Subcommittee on the Constitution, U.S. Senate Judiciary Committee, July 15, 1981.
2. Based on interviews with former Senate staffers who requested their identities not be revealed.
3. Ibid.
4. Ibid.
5. Ibid.
6. "Senator Clifford Case (R-N.J.): A Profile On His Record On Israel and Related Matters." (Prepared by Case's staff), 1978.
7. Ibid.
8. Ibid.
9. Ibid.
10. Ibid.
11. Ibid.
12. Addendum to January 7 Memorandum, Steve Bryen to Clifford Case, January 15, 1975.
13. Memorandum Of Steve Bryen to Clifford Case, January 7, 1975.
14. Ibid.
15. Ibid.
16. Ibid.
17. Ibid.
18. Memorandum "Shifting U.S. Policy in the Middle East?" Steven Bryen to Clifford P. Case, March 18, 1977.
19. Memorandum "Pressure and Threats Against Israel," Steven Bryen, October 4, 1977.
20. Memorandum "Middle East Negotiations" Steve Bryen to Members, Subcomittee On Near Eastern and South Asian Affairs, January 11, 1978.
21. Memorandum "The Coming War In The Middle East," Steve Bryen to Clifford P. Case, February 16, 1978.
22. "Statement to the U.S Senate," Richard Stone, February 27, 1978.
23. Memorandum, Stephen Bryen to Clifford P. Case, undated, [names crossed-out, but legible]
    See Appendix B

Chapter 6

1. "Action Memorandum," John H. Davitt, Chief,
   Internal Security Section, U.S. Department of
   Justice, to Philip B. Heymann, Assistant Attorney
   General, January 26, 1979.
   See Appendix C
2. Memorandum of Assistant Attorney General
   Benjamin R. Civiletti to William H. Webster,
   Director of Federal Bureau of Investigation, April
   26, 1978.
   See Appendix D
3. Letter of Douglas Wood, Chief, Freedom of
   Information/Privacy
   Unit, Criminal Division, U.S. Department of
   Justice, December 28, 1982.
   See Appendix E
4. Letter of Robert R. Belair, Esq., to Jonathan C.
   Rose, Assistant Attorney General, U.S.
   Department of Justice, January 31, 1983.
5. Based on interviews with confidential sources.
6. Martindale-Hubbard Law Directory, District of
   Columbia Sector, Under Miller, Cassidy, Larocca
   & Lewin.
7. Based on interviews with confidential sources.
8. Letter of Nathan Lewin, Esq., to Heymann,
   September 25, 1978.
9. Memorandum, Pending Cases, Registration Unit,
   Department of Justice, undated.
10. Letter of Lewin to Davitt, May 15, 1978.
11. Ibid.
12. Ibid.
13. Ibid.
14. Letter of Lewin to Heymann, September 25, 1978.
15. Memorandum from The Director, Defense
    Security Assistance Agency, Department of
    Defense, prepared by Colonel R.F. Ventrella,
    Middle East/Africa Division, undated.
16. Letter of Lewin to Heymann, September 25, 1978.
17. Ibid.
18. Memorandum of Ronald A. Stern, Special
    Assistant to the Assistant Attorney General, to
    Heymann, October 12, 1978.
    See Appendix F

19. Memorandum of Lisker to Davitt, September 26, 1979.
   See Appendix G
20. Letter of Senator Richard Stone to the Honorable Harold Brown, Secretary of Defense, February 23, 1978.
21. Letter of David E. McGiffort, Assistant Secretary of Defense, International Security Affairs, to Senator Stone, March 24, 1978.
22. See Lewin Letter to Davitt, May 15, 1978; and *Washington Post*, April 6, 1978; and *Rocky Mountain News*, April 9, 1978.
23. Stern Memorandum to Heymann, October 12, 1978.
   See Appendix F
24. Letter of Douglas S. Wood to Belair, May 4, 1983; attached as Schedule of Documents Denied.
25. Letter of Lewin to Heymann, September 25, 1978.
26. Memorandum of Stern to Heymann, October 12, 1978.
   See Appendix F
27. Ibid.
28. Letter of Edward M. Collins, Defense Intelligence Agency, to Timothy D. Mahoney, Agent, FBI, November 20, 1979; Attachment "The Intelligence Impact of the Unauthorized Disclosure to Israel of The DOD Analysis of the Saudi Arabian Request to Purchase F-15 Fighter Aircraft'."
   See Appendix H
29. Ibid.
30. Ibid.
31. Memorandum of Davitt to Lisker, November 24, 1978.
32. Letter of Davitt to Lewin, December 27, 1978.
33. Ibid.
34. Ibid.
35. Letter of Lewin to Davitt, January 17, 1979.
36. Action Memorandum of Davitt to Heymann, January 26, 1979.
   See Appendix C
37. Memorandum of Heymann to Bob Keuch, January 26, 1979.
38. Memorandum of Stern to Heymann and Keuch, January 26, 1979.
39. Letter of Lewin to Heymann, September 6, 1979.

40. Letter of Heyman to Lisker, signed by Keuch, May 25, 1975.
41. Letter of Lewin to Heymann, September 6, 1979.
42. Ibid.
43. Letter of Heymann to William B. Bader, Staff Director, U.S. Senate Committee on Foreign Relations, June 5, 1979.
44. *Defense Week*, June 20, 1983.
45. Memorandum of Joel Lisker, August 16, 1979.
46. Lewin Letter to Heymann, September 6, 1979.
47. Memorandum of Lisker, August 16, 1979.
48. Lewin Letter of September 6, 1979.
49. Ibid.
50. Memorandum of Lisker to Davitt, September 26, 1979.
    See Appendix H
51. Memorandum of Lisker, October 23, 1979.
    See Appendix I
52. Routing Slip, Author Unidentified, to "REK" (Robert E. Keuch) dated "10/10".
53. Routing Slip of Davitt to Heymann, dated "10/15".
54. Memorandum of Lisker to Davitt, November 9, 1979.
55. Memorandum of Robert A. McConnell, Assistant Attorney General, Office of Legislative Affairs, to Rudolph W. Giuliani, Associate Attorney General, undated.
56. Based on interviews of confidential sources.
57. Ibid.
58. Ibid.
59. Ibid.
60. Ibid.
61. Ibid.
62. Ibid.
63. Ibid.
64. Ibid.
65. Ibid.
66. Ibid.
67. Ibid.
68. For Philip B. Heymann resume, see Justice Department Press Release announcing his appointment to Assistant Attorney General, March 29, 1978. For Lewin's resume, see Martindale-Hubbell Law Directory, District of Columbia Section. Under Miller, Cassidy, Larroca & Lewin.

Chapter 7

1. *Air Force Magazine*, December 1982.
2. *Washington Post*, November 28, 1981.
3. *New York Times*, April 17, 1983.
4. Ibid.
5. Ibid.
6. *New York Times*, April 18, 1983.
7. Based on interviews with confidential sources.
8. *New York Times*, April 17, 1983.
9. *St. Louis Post-Dispatch*, April 20, 1983.
10. *New York Times*, April 21, 1983.
11. *Boston Globe*, April 23, 1983.
12. *Wall Street Journal*, June 24, 1983.
13. UPI, April 18, 1983.

Chapter 8

1. *Saudi Gazette*, June 16, 1982.
2. Ibid.
3. *The Technology Transfer Control Program: A Report to the 98th Congress*, Department of Defense, February 1983.
4. *JINSA Newsletter*, July 1981.
5. Ibid.
6. Ibid.
7. *JINSA Newsletter*, November 1982.
8. *JINSA Newsletter*, April 1983.
9. *Jewish Week*, August 12-18, 1982.
10. Ibid.
11. *JINSA Newsletter*, November 1982.
12. Ibid.
13. Ibid.
14. Ibid.
15. "Transfer of U.S. High-Technology to the Soviet Union": Hearing Before the Permanent Subcommittee on Investigations of the Committee of Governmental Affairs, U.S. Senate, 97th Congress, Second Session; May 4, 5, 6, 11, 12, 1982 page 255.
16. *JINSA Newsletter*, June-July, 1982.
17. Ibid.
18. Ibid.
19. *JINSA Newsletter*, November 1982.
20. Ibid.

21. Ibid.
22. *JINSA Newsletter*, April, 1982.
23. Ibid.
24. *JINSA Newsletter*, November 1983.
25. *New York Times*, July 6, 1983.
26. *JINSA Newsletter*, July-August 1983.

Chapter 9

1. *New York Times*, July 10, 1983.
2. *U.S. Assistance to the State of Israel*, U.S. General Accounting Office, June 24, 1983.
3. Ibid.
4. *Draft of Proposed Report on U.S. Assistance to the State of Israel*, prepared by the staff of the U.S. General Accounting Office.
5. Ibid.
6. Ibid.
7. Ibid.
8. Ibid.
9. Ibid.
10. Ibid.
11. Ibid.
12. Ibid.
13. Ibid.
14. Ibid.
15. Ibid.
16. Ibid.
17. Ibid.
18. Ibid.
19. Ibid.
20. Ibid.
21. *JINSA Newsletter*, November 1983.
22. Ibid.

Chapter 10

1. Testimony of Dr. Stephen D. Bryen, Deputy Assistant Secretary of Defense, International Economic, Trade and Security Policy, Department of Defense, before the Permanent Subcommittee on Investigations, U.S. Committee on Governmental Affairs, May 1982.
2. *The Technology Transfer Control Program*, op cited.
3. *Journal of Electronic Defense*, May 1983.

4. Ibid.
5. Ibid.
6. *Aviation Week*, December 19, 1983.
7. Ibid.
8. Ibid.
9. Ibid.
10. Department of Defense, *The Technology Control Program:* Report to the 98th Congress, second session, February 1984.
11. Ibid.
12. Ibid.
13. Ibid.
14. Ibid.
15. Open letter to the President and Congress, William A. Root, former director of State Department Office of East-West Trade, September 24, 1983.
16. Ibid.
17. Ibid.
18. Ibid.
19. Ibid.
20. *Washington Post*, September 26, 1983.
21. Ibid.
22. *New York Times*, September 26, 1983.
23. Letter to the Editor of the *New York Times*, September 27, 1983, William A. Root, unpublished.
24. Ibid.
25. *Washington Post*, May 10, 1983.
26. Internal Commerce Department Memo, undated.
27. Ibid.
28. *The Washington Post*, March 24, 1984.
29. Ibid.
30. *Washington Post*, April 12, 1984.
31. Ibid.
32. *Washington Post*, April 11, 1984.
33. Ibid.
34. *Washington Post*, March 19, 1984.
35. Ibid.
36. Ibid.

Chapter 11

1. General Accounting Office Report, *U.S. Assistance to the State of Israel*, op cit.

2. "Israel: Foreign Intelligence and Security Services" report prepared by the U.S. Central Intelligence Agency, March 1979.
3. *The Listener*, March 8, 1984.
4. Ibid.
5. Ibid.
6. Press Notice, Britsh Department of Trade and Industry, March 6, 1984.
7. Ibid.
8. Confidencial source.
9. *The Spotlight*, March 5, 1984.
10. *The Washington Post*, January 1, 1984.
11. Confidential source.
12. *The Rockford Register - Star*, August 18, 1983.
13. *The Jerusalem Post*, February 12-18, 1984.
14. *Israel's Foreign Trade '82*, Ministry of Industry and Trade.
15. *The Israel Economist*, August 1983.
16. *The New York Times*, April 22, 1984.
17. Testimony of Richard N. Perle, Assistant Secretary of Defense, before the Senate Committee on Government Affairs, Permanent Subcommittee on Investigations, April 11, 1984.
18. Ibid.
19. Ibid.
20. Ibid.
21. Ibid.
22. *The Jerusalem Post*, April 1-7, 1984.
23. Ibid.
24. Ibid.
25. Ibid.
26. Ibid.
27. *Dallas Morning News*, March 21, 1982.
28. Letter of John W. Dixon to Secretary of Defense Caspar Weinberger, February 12, 1982.
29. *Dallas Morning News*, March 21, 1982.
30. *Foreign Economic Trends and Their Implications for the United States: Israel*, September 1983, U.S. Department of Commerce, International Trade Administration, FET 83-059.
31. *Jerusalem Post*, January 29 - February 4, 1984.
32. Ibid.
33. Confidential source.
34. *Washington Post*, May 6, 1984.
35. Ibid.
36. Ibid.
37. Ibid.

Chapter 12

1. *New York Times*, October 25, 1983.
2. Ibid.
3. *New York Times*, November 27, 1983.
4. *New York Times*, November 29, 1983.
5. *New York Times*, December 16, 1983.
6. *New York Times*, November 30, 1983.
7. *Washington Post*, December 23, 1983.
8. *The New York Times*, March 15, 1984.
9. Ibid.
10. Ibid.
11. Jack Anderson, *The Washington Post*, December 20, 1984.
12. Ibid.
13. Ibid.
14. *The New York Times*, January 15, 1984.
15. Interview with confidential source.

Conclusion

1. *Journal of Electronic Defense*, May 1983.
2. *New York Times*, December 4, 1977.
3. Testimony of Richard N. Perle, Assistant Secretary of Defense, before the Special Panel on Arms Control and Disarmament, House Armed Services Committee, July 14, 1983.
4. Remarks of Ronald Reagan in White House meeting with religious leaders, April 7, 1983.
5. *Monitin*, July 1983.
6. Ibid.
7. *Washington Post*, October 18, 1983.
8. Interview of business executive who wishes to remain confidential.
9. *Washington Post*.
10. Ibid.
11. *Washington Post*, April 8, 1984.
12. Ibid.
13. *New York Times*, April 17, 1983.

LIST OF ACRONYMS:

ADC	American-Arab Anti-Discrimination Committee
AIPAC	American-Israeli Public Affairs Committee
CIA	(U.S.) Central Intelligence Agency
COCOM	Coordinating Committee for Multilateral Export Controls
DIA	(U.S.) Defense Intelligence Agency
DOD	(U.S.) Department of Defense
DOJ	(U.S.) Department of Justice
ECI	Electronic Corporation of Israel
ECM	Electronic counter-measures
FBI	(U.S.) Federal Bureau of Investigation
FOIA	Freedom of Information Act
FORDTIS	Foreign Disclosure and Technical Information System
GAO	(U.S.) General Accounting Office
JINSA	Jewish Institute for National Security Affairs
MOU	Memorandum of Understanding
NAAA	National Association of Arab-Americans
NATO	North Atlantic Treaty Organization
PLO	Palestine Liberation Organization
SEC	(U.S.) Security and Exchange Commission
VHSIC	Very-High-Speed Integrated Circuits

APPENDIX

A. Affidavit of Michael P. Saba. Cited in Chapter 1, note 1.

B. Memo of Stephen Bryen to Senator Case. Cited in Chapter 5, note 23.

C. Action Memorandum of John H. Davitt, Chief, Internal Security Section, Criminal Division, to Philip B. Heymann, Assistant Attorney General, Criminal Division, January 26, 1979. Cited in Chapter 6, note 1.

D. Memo of Benjamin R. Civiletti, Assistant Attorney General, Criminal Division, to Director of the FBI, April 26, 1978. Cited in Chapter 6, note 2.

E. Letter of Douglas S. Wood, Chief, Freedom of Information/ Privacy Act Unit, Criminal Division, to J.R. AbiNader, National Association of Arab Americans, 28 December 1982. Cited in Chapter 6, note 3.

F. Memo of Ronald A. Stern, Special Assistant to the Assistant Attorney General, Criminal Division to Philip B. Heymann, Assistant Attorney General, Criminal Division. Cited in Chapter 6, note 18.

G. Memo of Joel S. Lisker, Chief, Registration Unit, Internal Security Section, to John H. Davitt, Chief, Internal Security Section, Criminal Division, September 26, 1979. Cited in Chapter 6, note 19.

H. Letter of Edward M. Collins, Defense Intelligence Agency, to FBI Washington Field Office, Attn: Timothy Mahoney, 20 November 1978, with Attachment DIA analysis of "The Intelligence Impact of the Unauthorized Disclosure to Israel of the 'DOD Analysis of the Saudi Arabian Request to Purchase F-15 Fighter Aircraft.' " Cited in Chapter 6, note 37.

I. Memo of Joel S. Lisker, Chief, Registration Unit, Criminal Division, to Files, October 23, 1979. Cited in Chapter 6, note 51.

AFFIDAVIT OF MICHAEL P. SABA

My name is Michael P. Saba. I am President of Development International, Inc., an international trade organization based in North Dakota. I am also a Director of International Agricultural Development Pool, a non-profit body which is coordinating international agricultural activities. I am an American of Middle Eastern ancestory, and I was formerly, from August 1976, to August 1977, the Executive Director of the National Association of Arab-Americans. My previous activities and employments have involved the United States Peace Corps, educational consultant, university research assistant, education development coordinator, and North Dakota State training director and civil rights officer.

The following represents my sworn affidavit with respect to events which occurred on the morning of March 9, 1978, Washington, D. C.

On the morning of March 9, 1978, I went to the Madison Hotel for an early morning business meeting. I arrived at approximately 8:30 and went to the Coffee House off of the main lobby of the Madison. This is the coffee house which has glass doors from which one can see out into the corridor. As I entered, a hostess escorted me to a seat in a corner, where I was facing toward the desk where the cashier sits. As I followed the hostess I passed a table where several gentlemen were sitting.

I was seated immediately adjacent to the table where the gentlemen were sitting, and I was approximately six or seven feet away from the closest gentleman whose back was to me, and about ten or twelve feet from a gentleman who was facing me. As I sat down I recognized the gentleman facing me, with a mous-

Affidavit of Michael P. Saba. Cited in Chapter 1, Note 1.

- 2 -

tache, as being familiar to me, but I did not immediately place him. At that time I thought no more about it, and commenced to read the morning paper which I had with me.

I did not pay much attention to the group until another gentleman came and joined the table. When the next gentleman came in, the whole group stood up and began to greet each other in Hebrew. I am quite sure it was Hebrew, since I noticed the word Shalom, and I have heard Hebrew spoken many times.

When the new gentleman came to the table the man who looked familiar to me was specifically introduced by the man on his left as "Mr. Stephen Bryen of the Senate Foreign Relations Committee." At this point I recognized Steve Bryen as a staff employee of the Senate Foreign Relations Committee. I had had some exposure to him when I was on Capitol Hill as an employee of the National Association of Arab-Americans. The man who was providing the introductions spoke English very well, without any noticeable accent. Thus, I heard the introduction quite clearly.

Two of the gentlemen began to speak Hebrew again, and at that point I became more interested in the conversation. As an American of Middle Eastern ancestry, I was of course curious as to what an employee of the Senate Foreign Relations Committee was talking about with what appeared to be Israeli citizens.

They all sat down at this point, and there was a clear space through which I could directly see and hear Steve Bryen. I was approximately ten or twelve feet away from him at this point, and his voice was very clear. I could hear almost everything he was saying. At this point I would estimate it was approximately 8:45 to 8:50 when the group began the discussion to which I was a witness.

- 3 -

At first they were discussing Ezer Weizman and his trip to this country. I recognized Weizman's name as being that of the Israeli Defense Minister, and I knew he was visiting this country. They also were generally discussing Prime Minister Begin, and his anticipated arrival. The conversation indicated that some of the men appeared to be part of an advance team or assistants to Defense Minister Weizman or Prime Minister Begin. Clearly they were associated with the Israeli government, and not members of the American Jewish community. As the conversation progressed I thought that it was quite important for me to listen carefully, and if possible to take notes. The tone of the discussion took on that of a strategy session which Mr. Bryen was leading. He appeared to be advising the Israelis on a strategy of how to deal with the current Israeli-Arab conflict, insofar as the current Administration was concerned. At this point I took out some small pieces of paper that I had in my pocket and began to write notes directly from some of the things that Mr. Bryen was saying.

It struck me that they were not merely discussing the Arab-Israeli conflict, or American public opinion, in general terms, but rather with the specific intention of devising of strategy of how this Israeli delegation could affect United States foreign policy determinations. Bryen quite clearly, to me, was outlining what their policy and strategy should be.

What really surprised me at this point was the fact that an employee of the United States government Foreign Relations Committee was using the pronoun "we" to embrace his own position and that of the Israelis, and the pronoun "they" to describe the Carter Administration and the U. S. Government's position. Bryen continually referred to the group collectively as "we." An example would be

- 4 -

"We must tell the Administration this;" and "They are going to do this." In all uses of the pronoun "we" it was clear that he was referring to the Israelis and not to the Senate Foreign Relations Committee or the U. S. Government. He continually referred to the U. S. Government, President Carter, Brzezinski and various U. S. Senators as "they."

Since I was not able to write everything down, I did try accurately to record the most interesting quotes, as well as the general thread of conversation. The bulk of the conversation was in English, and thus presented no difficulty in being heard or understood. Immediately after the meeting broke up, I transferred my notes to a larger paper, so that they were very fresh in my mind at the time I recorded them.

From approximately 8:50 to 9:20 the group discussed what Israel must do to maintain control in the U. S. Congress, what must be done concerning the National Security Council.

Bryen led a discussion to the effect that the Israelis were losing a lot of credibility with the Congress and the Administration, and that the loss of this credibility appeared to stem directly from Prime Minister Begin's insistence on a religious and historical justification for maintaining the West Bank. It was Bryen's feeling, that he articulated quite clearly, that the Israelis were losing credibility by pushing this argument and that they had to change their argument. At this point he said specifically:

"We must re-establish credibility."

"We're missing an opportunity right now."

- 5 -

He then stated that Prime Minister Begin had "missed the boat." It was Bryen's position that the way to keep the West Bank for the Israelis, was through the argument that its retention was compelled for security reasons. At this point, referring to the U. S. Administration he said:

"Get them to save their credibility."

It appeared that he was talking about the Administration's credibility with the American Jewish community concerning statements that have recently been made by the Administration.

Bryen began talking about what needed to be done with Congress and what Congress would accept as a valid argument for justifying a retention of the West Bank by Israel. There appeared to be some disagreement, and some of the Israelis apparently were arguing that pushing the religious and historical claim to the West Bank was a legitimate strategy. Bryen rejected this out of hand and stated:

"The West Bank can be gained on security grounds."

"To get Jackson and the others back, we must push the security issue."

His references in this context were apparently to the fact that several Israeli supporters were disenchanted by Israel's claim to the West Bank on religious or historical grounds, but that they could be "brought back" if the Israeli government were to push forth its claim on "security grounds," exclusively.

They then began discussing Weizman's arrival, and what Weizman had already said. Bryen saw Weizman's arrival as an opportunity to shift public opinion in this country. Bryen said:

"There should be a statement from Weizman right now on suspension of the settlements."

- 6 -

There was then some discussion about the settlements. It appeared that the Israeli delegation was asking questions about why Begin's arguments were so ineffective and Bryen responded:

"This is the only argument [security grounds] that would help us to keep the West Bank, and we must push it, and we must get people like Weizman to make a statement at this point."

Bryen was asked about some Israeli statements that had recently been made concerning the settlements and he responded:

"When an order was given to stop it [referring to further settlements] it was stopped, but the State Department made no reaction at all."

"We've got to get this to the press."

They then began to discuss the Administration and what the President had said and done, and this was about one-third of the way through the conversation, and Bryen said:

"Never let the President of the United States get away with these kinds of statements."

He was apparently referring to what he felt the delegation should do in response to recent statements by President Carter concerning the West Bank. There then followed some general discussion about Carter, Brzezinski and others by name. At this point Bryen said:

"This Administration is so pig headed that we have to deal differently."

It was at this point that Brzezinski's name came up specifically, and there was some discussion about him. Bryen then said:

"One of the saddest things is what they did to Mark Siegel. Brzezinski set him up."

It was at this point that another gentleman joined the group. He was an impressive looking man, rather stately, about 5 foot 10, with reddish thin hair. He appeared to be fairly important since the whole group rose when he came and shook hands and seemed quite deferential. This gentleman mentioned something about going to Watergate. Most of the conversation at this point was in Hebrew. I do not know whether Bryen was following the conversation, although he did at one point say Shalom.

At this point they began to talk about Congress and the arms issues. In a general discussion of the Administration's position on the proposed sale of planes to Saudia Arabia, Egypt and Israel, Bryen said:

> "They think they have Church, and have neutralized Jackson, but Henry wouldn't make a deal without talking to us about it."

Some discussion continued about their strategy for dealing with the arms, and Bryen said:

> "We must do something in May, so that we have done what they have asked, that way we can get back Jackson and the liberals then we'll build momentum."

Then the discussion went clearly into the arms sales where they began to talk about arms, airplanes, and at this point there was some mention about the Sparrow from Britain.

The delegation then began to talk about how they could get the arms they wanted, and Bryen said:

> "We can make them bargain."

At this point in response to a request as to whether certain information was available Bryen said:

"I have the Pentagon document on the bases, which you are welcome to see."

The group then commenced to talk about Brzezinski and the National Security Council. Bryen said:

"We need to get inside the bargain with Brzezinski."

"The main thing to do is to make a deal in the National Security Council."

There followed more references and discussions about the weapons and about the sale of airplanes to Egypt, Saudia Arabia and Israel. At this point, after the Israeli delegation discussed the weapons which they needed, Bryen said:

"I hope you have good R & D [apparently Research and Development] and get ready to convert it into weapons."

There followed a general discussion as to how they would get into the National Security Council. Bryen said:

"We should play for the compromise."

Then after some discussion on strategy as to how to play for this compromise, Bryen stated:

"Our best bet now is Erich von Marbod, he's the military sales guy on the deal...he looks German but he's with us."

There was then some discussion at this point as most of the people did not know exactly who Bryen was referring to.

They then talked about the proposed sale of aircraft to the Saudis, the Egyptians and the Israeli portion. Bryen then said:

"We can't stop the Egyptian part."

and then made some reference to being able to stop the sale of aircraft to the Saudis.

- 9 -

Bryen in conversation about airplanes, said "Its not a bad airplane, I've flown it myself, or I've flown in it myself." I did not know which airplane he was referring to.

Shortly afterwards Bryen said, referring to some airplane or weapons system, although I think he was referring to an airplane,

"Can you make it yourself?"

and was answered

"Yes, we don't have to buy it."

Bryen said:

"Good then we're all right there."

At this point the conversation drifted into social amentities and Bryen said "I've got to get back to the Hill." The group then left the coffee house, with the Israeli group moving toward the lobby, and Bryen out to the newstand. The time was approximately 9:45 a.m. I had written these things down on little pieces of paper as they were being said, and I sat there and collected my thoughts, and transcribed my notes into a more comprehensive fashion.

The foregoing represents my true and complete recollection of the events which occurred, and all of the matters contained are true and correct to the best of my knowledge.

Michael P. Saba
Michael P. Saba

On this _13th_ day of March, 1978,
the aforesaid Michael P. Saba did
appear before me, and attest, under
oath, that the above represented his
sworn statement.

Notary Public

My Commission Expires:

To: ~~Senator Case~~
From: ~~S. Bryen~~

    The administration appears deeply shaken by the House International Relations Committee action last evening in which 22 Members agreed to cosponsor a resolution of disapproval against all the Arms sales.

    The administration has <u>no</u> vote count on a blanket disapproval and they will be discovering today that they do not have the votes to overcome a blanket turndown.

    Therefore, the administration will offer a "compromise," if they can get takers. The substance of the compromise will be <u>more</u> airplanes for Israel.

    The now "famous" meeting I had at the Madison with Israel's top man in the Defense Ministry had as its basic conclusion the following pertinent information regarding Israel's aircraft purchases.

    (1) Israel cannot afford to pay for more airplanes.

    (2) Israel cannot afford to buy the 75 F-16's offered to her in the package.

    (3) It is <u>unlikely that Israel</u> will be able to purchase any more than 50 F-16's by 1980-1981.

    (4) The administration is aware fully that Israel cannot afford the additional airplanes. and does not plan to offer more military assistance to make it possible for her to purchase more. The administration also cut off the possibility of coproduction of the F-16, which would have lowered per unit costs and made it financially possible for Israel to buy more planes.

    (5) The Budget Committee will not authorize any more security supporting assistance funds this year so the chance to increase funds for Israel to enable her to buy more aircraft is out of the question.

This is the essence of the problem created by the arms sale and the "search" for a compromise. The sixty planes for Saudi Arabia is just two much to deal with, more than two times too much under the circumstances. In consideration of any "compromise," these are the key salient facts to have in mind.

Memo of Stephen Bryen to Senator Case. Cited in Chapter 5, Note 23.

UNITED STATES GOVERNMENT

memorandum

DATE: January 26, 1979
REPLY TO ATTN OF: John H. Davitt, Chief
Internal Security Section
Criminal Division

SUBJECT: Stephen David Bryen
Foreign Agents Registration Act - Israel
Conflict of Interest; Espionage - Israel

TO: Philip B. Heymann
Assistant Attorney General
Criminal Division

ACTION MEMORANDUM

The purpose of this memorandum is to provide you with an update of events in this investigation since our meeting of December 19, 1978 with Bob Keuch and Ron Stern. At that meeting we discussed some of the unresolved questions in the case. We agreed that the investigation could not be terminated and that there were three options open to us in order to resolve these questions.

The first option was to bring the matter before an investigative grand jury. The second was to accept all of the conditions and limitations imposed by Lewin and to proceed with the interview. The third option was to accede to some of Lewin's conditions and request that Bryen be made available for interview.

We agreed that we would adopt option three and present Lewin with a counter proposal which, if agreeable to Bryen, would allow us to proceed with the interview. This compromise was set forth in our letter of December 27, 1978 to Lewin. At that time he was furnished with a list of areas of inquiry which would be put to his client in the form of questions. In his response of January 17, 1979 Lewin "totally rejected" the proposal that the investigation include Bryen's interview (page 2 penultimate paragraph). This refusal leaves but two alternatives, only one of which is viable.

The first option is discontinue further investigation as it now stands thus leaving many unanswered questions. (We have not considered another letter or telephone call to Lewin as an option because Lewin makes quite clear in

cc: Mr. Keuch
    Mr. Stern

Buy U.S. Savings Bonds Regularly on the Payroll Savings Plan

OPTIONAL FORM NO. 10
(REV. 7-76)
GSA FPMR (41 CFR) 101-11.6
5010-112

*U.S. Government Printing Office: 1977—241-530/6496

Action Memorandum of John H. Davitt, Chief, Internal Security Section, Criminal Division, to Philip B. Heymann, Assistant Attorney General, Criminal Division, January 26, 1974. Cited in Chapter 6, Note 1.

- 2 -

his letter that unless we agree to all of his conditions,
including limiting our areas of inquiry, he will not assent
to an interview of his client; thus his "total rejection"
of our offer). The second option and the one which we urge
strongly is to complete this important inquiry before an
investigative grand jury. Some of the unresolved questions
thus far, which suggest that Bryen is (a) gathering classified
information for the Israelis, (b) acting as their unregistered
agent and (c) lying about it, are as follows:

5
6
7c

(Author's Note: Information deleted by the U.S. Government)

- 3 -

(Author's Note: Information deleted by the U.S. Government)

(Author's Note: Information deleted by the U.S. Government)

(Author's Note: Information deleted by the U.S. Government)

(Author's Note: Information deleted by the U.S. Government)

(Author's Note: Information deleted by the U.S. Government)

- 8 -

Recommendation

Based on the foregoing, we recommend that this matter
be presented to a federal grand jury sitting in Washington,
D.C.

_____
Date

_____
Approved

_____
Date

_____
Disapproved

Joel S. Lisker
724-7109

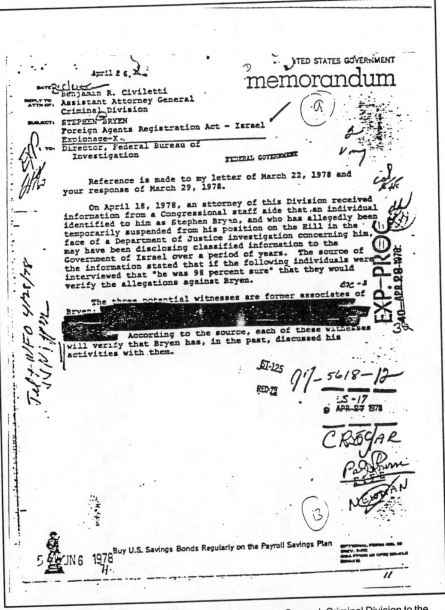

April 26, 1978

DATE:
REPLY TO
ATTN OF: Benjamin R. Civiletti
Assistant Attorney General
Criminal Division

SUBJECT: STEPHEN BRYEN
Foreign Agents Registration Act – Israel
Espionage-X

TO: Director, Federal Bureau of
Investigation

UNITED STATES GOVERNMENT
memorandum

Reference is made to my letter of March 22, 1978 and
your response of March 29, 1978.

On April 18, 1978, an attorney of this Division received
information from a Congressional staff aide that an individual
identified to him as Stephen Bryen, and who has allegedly been
temporarily suspended from his position on the Hill in the
face of a Department of Justice investigation concerning him,
may have been disclosing classified information to the
Government of Israel over a period of years. The source of
the information stated that if the following individuals were
interviewed that "he was 98 percent sure" that they would
verify the allegations against Bryen.

The three potential witnesses are former associates of
Bryen:
_____
According to the source, each of these witnesses
will verify that Bryen has, in the past, discussed his
activities with them.

Buy U.S. Savings Bonds Regularly on the Payroll Savings Plan

Memorandum of Benjamin R. Civiletti, Assistant Attorney General, Criminal Division to the
Director of the FBI, April 26, 1978. Cited in Chapter 6, Note 2.

(Author's Note: Information Blacked Out by the U.S. Government)

U.S. Department of Justice

RECEIVED DEC 3 0 1982

CRM-6212-F

Washington, D.C. 20530

2 8 DEC 1982

Mr. J. R. AbiNader
National Association of Arab
  Americans
1825 Connecticut Avenue, N.W.
Washington, D.C. 20009

Dear Mr. AbiNader:

This is in response to your request of April 25, 1980, for
access to records concerning Stephen D. Bryen.

A search of the Criminal Division's central index revealed
that there were records within the scope of your request in the Internal
Security Section. After an exhaustive search, however, these records
could not be located. Fortunately the attorney responsible for this
matter kept a "working file" which should contain most of the records
contained in the original. There is no way, however, to identify what
records, if any, were missing.

The file contained 39 records originated by the Criminal
Division. Items 1 through 23 are being released in their entirety.
Items 24 through 33 are being released also, but with deletions. Items
34 through 39, described on the attached schedule, are being withheld.
The Freedom of Information Act exemptions which apply to items 24 through
39 are 5 U.S.C. 552(b)(1) (documents which are properly classified
pursuant to Executive Order); (3) (documents which are specifically
exempted from disclosure by statute (in this instance Rule 30 of the
United States Senate which states that no paper presented to the Senate
shall be withdrawn from its files except by order of the Senate; in the
alternative these records are congressional records rather than agency
ones and thus are not subject to the FOIA)); (5) (inter- or intra-agency
correspondence that is predecisional and reflects the deliberative
processes and/or attorney work product of the Department); (6) (documents
which if disclosed would constitute a clearly unwarranted invasion of
the personal privacy of a third party); (7) (investigatory records
compiled for law enforcement purposes which if disclosed would (C)
constitute an unwarranted invasion of the personal privacy of a third
party; and (D) disclose the identity of a confidential source or information
furnished solely by a confidential source).

Letter of Douglas S. Wood, Chief, Freedom of Information/Privacy Act Unit, Criminal
Division, to J. R. AbiNader, National Association of Arab Americans, 28 December 1982.
Cited in Chapter 6, Note 3.

- 2 -

You should note that in addition to the preceeding explanation items numbered 27 and 35 contain information which is outside the scope of your request. Alternatively, that information would have been deleted pursuant to 5 U.S.C. 552(b)(6) and (7)(C).

We also located documents which may pertain to your request which originated with the Department of State, Department of Defense, and the Federal Bureau of Investigation. Pursuant to Departmental practice we are referring those documents to their originating offices for review and direct reply to you.

Pursuant to Department regulations, you have a right to appeal this partial denial of your request. This appeal must be made within thirty days in writing and addressed to: Assistant Attorney General, Office of Legal Policy (Attention: Office of Information and Privacy) United States Department of Justice, Washington, D.C. 20530. The envelope and letter should be clearly marked, "FOIPA Appeal". If on appeal your request is denied, judicial review will thereafter be available to you in the district in which you reside or have your principal place of business or the district in which the records denied to you are located or the District of Columbia.

Sincerely,

DOUGLAS S. WOOD, Chief
Freedom of Information/Privacy Act Unit
Criminal Division

5/6/83

UNITED STATES GOVERNMENT

Memorandum

TO : Philip B. Heymann
Assistant Attorney General
Criminal Division

FROM : Ronald A. Stern
Special Assistant to the AAG
Criminal Division

SUBJECT: Stephen David Byren -- Investigation

DATE:

This memo will briefly summarize the matters under investigation involving Mr. Bryen and indicate the aspects that appear to be open matters of investigation at this time.

"Facts"

On March 9, 1978, Bryen met with several Israeli officials in the coffee shop of the Madison Hotel in Washington, D.C. A Mr. Michael P. Saba has provided the Department with an affidavit setting forth the substance of the conversation that he overheard from an adjacent table in the Madison coffee shop. Mr. Saba is former Executive Director of the National Association of Arab-Americans. Mr. Saba's March 13 affidavit stated that the discussion between Bryen and the Israelis had the tone of a strategy session which Bryen appeared to be directing. According to Saba, Bryen spoke in terms of what "we" (himself and the Israelis) had to do to influence "them" (the Carter Administration) on Middle East policy. One allegedly verbatim statement set forth in the affidavit has Bryen stating to the Israelis that he had "the Pentagon document on the bases," which the Israelis were welcome to see. The affidavit suggests that Bryen may be acting as an agent of the Israeli government and that Bryen may be providing Israeli officials with classified documents (these suggestions are not stated as express accusations but are implicit from the substance of the affidavit).

In addition, in April 1978, George Calhoun received a call from a source who requested confidentiality.

(7)(D)

Buy U.S. Savings Bonds Regularly on the Payroll Savings Plan

Form OBD-197
MAY 1978

Memorandum of Ronald A. Stern, Special Assistant to the Assistant Attorney General, Criminal Division, to Philip B. Heymann, Assistant Attorney General, Criminal Division. Cited in Chapter 6, Note 18.

(Author's Note: Information Blacked Out by the U.S. Government)

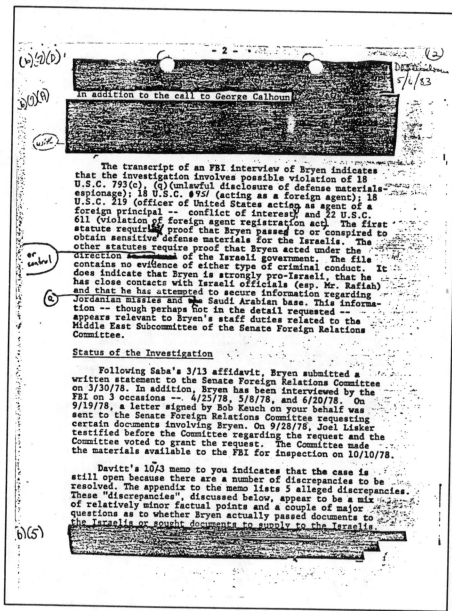

(b)(2)(D)

(b)(2)(A)

(with)

- 2 -

(2)

5/6/83

In addition to the call to George Calhoun

The transcript of an FBI interview of Bryen indicates that the investigation involves possible violation of 18 U.S.C. 793(c), (q)(unlawful disclosure of defense materials—espionage); 18 U.S.C. #951 (acting as a foreign agent); 18 U.S.C. 219 (officer of United States acting as agent of a foreign principal -- conflict of interest); and 22 U.S.C. 611 (violation of foreign agent registration act). The first statute requires proof that Bryen passed to or conspired to obtain sensitive defense materials for the Israelis. The other statutes require proof that Bryen acted under the direction and control of the Israeli government. The file contains no evidence of either type of criminal conduct. It does indicate that Bryen is strongly pro-Israeli, that he has close contacts with Israeli officials (esp. Mr. Rafiah) and that he has attempted to secure information regarding Jordanian missiles and the Saudi Arabian base. This information -- though perhaps not in the detail requested -- appears relevant to Bryen's staff duties related to the Middle East Subcommittee of the Senate Foreign Relations Committee.

or control

Q

Status of the Investigation

Following Saba's 3/13 affidavit, Bryen submitted a written statement to the Senate Foreign Relations Committee on 3/30/78. In addition, Bryen has been interviewed by the FBI on 3 occasions --. 4/25/78, 5/8/78, and 6/20/78. On 9/19/78, a letter signed by Bob Keuch on your behalf was sent to the Senate Foreign Relations Committee requesting certain documents involving Bryen. On 9/28/78, Joel Lisker testified before the Committee regarding the request and the Committee voted to grant the request. The Committee made the materials available to the FBI for inspection on 10/10/78.

Davitt's 10/3 memo to you indicates that the case is still open because there are a number of discrepancies to be resolved. The appendix to the memo lists 5 alleged discrepancies. These "discrepancies", discussed below, appear to be a mix of relatively minor factual points and a couple of major questions as to whether Bryen actually passed documents to the Israelis or sought documents to supply to the Israelis.

b)(5)

(Author's Note: Information Blacked Out by the U.S. Government)

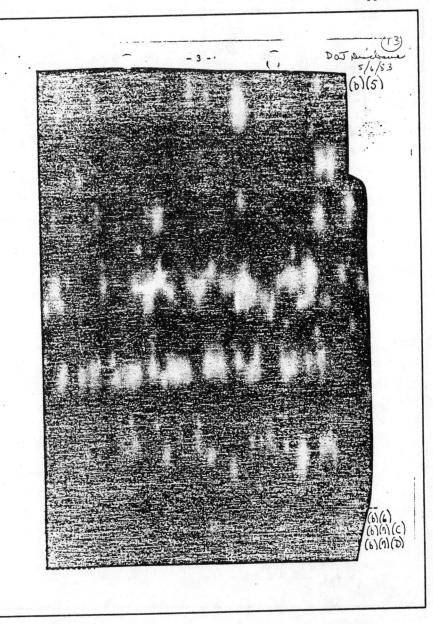

(Author's Note: Information Blacked Out by the U.S. Government)

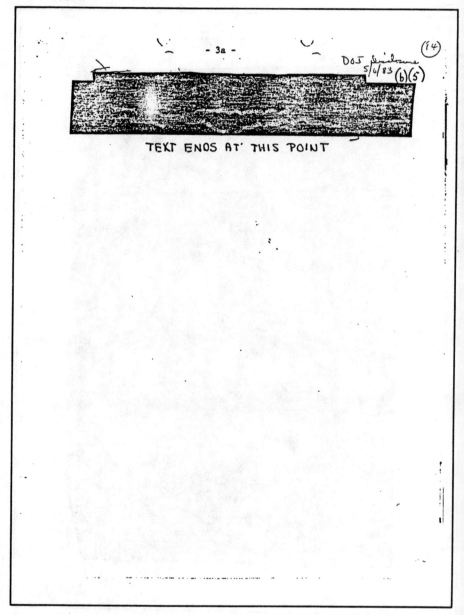

- 3a -

DOJ
5/6/83 (b)(5)

(14)

TEXT ENDS AT THIS POINT

(Author's Note: Information Blacked Out by the U.S. Government)

- 4 -

4. The 4th item concerns Saba's statement that he overheard Bryen state that he had a Pentagom document on bases that the Israelis are welcome to see. Bryen denies having any Pentagon document on bases or offering any Pentagon document to the Israelis. Saba has taken a polygraph and passed on the general validity of his affidavit but the polygraph was inconclusive on the specific Pentagon document statement. The FBI has found 9 latent prints of Bryen's on a classified DOD report on the Saudi Arabian request to purchase F-15s from the United States. This report was supplied to the Senate Foreign Relations Committee on 3/8/78 -- the day before the 3/9 meeting. That report, however, does not concern bases. Senator Stone (a member of the Committee) had requested a report on a Saudi base at Tabuk by letter of 2/23/78 but this request was refused by DOD on 3/24/78. It is not clear what report on bases Bryen could have had on 3/9, unless he found another means to secure the information on Tabuk.

"The Pentagon document" question is appropriately the key concern of Internal Security. There is no evidence that Bryen passed such a document or offered one to the Israelis other than Saba's affidavit. Bryen's fingerprints on the F-15 document are not very probative since Bryen would have reviewed this document as part of his staff function and since the document is not about "bases." There is no indication that Bryen obtain documents (if such exist) about Tabuk or had an incentive to try to do so while Senator Stone's report was pending. (Perhaps Bryen assumed he would get the Tabuk information since Stone had requested it. Bryen may have jumped the gun in his statement at the 3/9 meeting, assuming Saba's affidavit is correct). There are no additional investigative steps contemplated by Internal Security on this aspect of the affidavit at this time.

5. The 5th and final item concerns Bryen May 1977 request while in Amman Jordan for a map detailing the location of I-Hawk missles in Jordan with an indication of their range. The request was made of the US Ambassador in Jordan who had arranged for a briefing of Bryen while he was in Jordan. The request was cabled to DOD which determined that the material was very sensitive to Jordan and that Bryen did not have a need to know. The map was not forwarded to Bryen and he let the matter drop. This "discrepancy" appears to be based on Bryen's statement that in general when he wanted specific information he would make a written request.

The file reveals that the Committee has no procedure requiring staff members to obtain clearance to request sensitive information. Senator Stone does not recall authorizing Byren to make such a request but did not see anything wrong with the request. The Committee has recently written

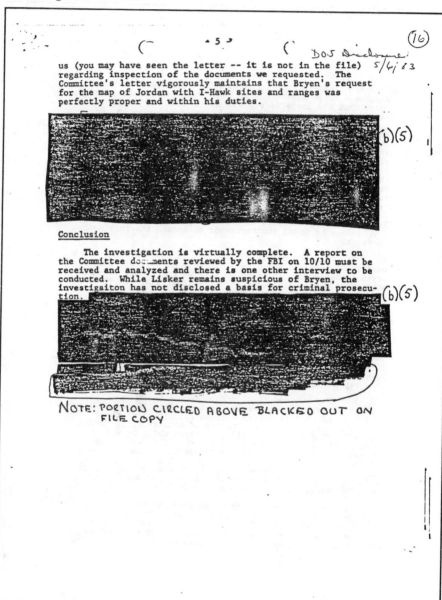

(16)

DoS Disclosure
5/4/83

us (you may have seen the letter -- it is not in the file)
regarding inspection of the documents we requested. The
Committee's letter vigorously maintains that Bryen's request
for the map of Jordan with I-Hawk sites and ranges was
perfectly proper and within his duties.

(b)(5)

Conclusion

The investigation is virtually complete. A report on
the Committee documents reviewed by the FBI on 10/10 must be
received and analyzed and there is one other interview to be
conducted. While Lisker remains suspicious of Bryen, the
investigaiton has not disclosed a basis for criminal prosecution.

(b)(5)

NOTE: PORTION CIRCLED ABOVE BLACKED OUT ON
FILE COPY

(Author's Note: Information Blacked Out by the U.S. Government)

G   DOJ Disclosure
5/6/83

⑧

UNITED STATES GOVERNMENT

Memorandum

TO : John H. Davitt, Chief
Internal Security Section
Criminal Division

DATE: September 26, 1979

JSL:mes
146-7-16-808

FROM : Joel S. Lisker, Chief
Registration Unit
Internal Security Section

SUBJECT: Status of our request for access to documents of the
Senate Foreign Relations Committee regarding STEPHEN
DAVID BRYEN

    This morning I called Patrick Shea at his request
for a status report on our request for access to certain
documents, including Department of Defense classified
materials, maintained by the Senate Foreign Relations
Committee.

    Shea told me that pursuant to the request of
Senators Javits and Church he met with the Legal Counsel
to the Senate on the subject of access to the documents
by former Senator Case, Stephen Bryen and his counsel
Nathan Lewin. This access is for the purpose of permitting
these individuals to review the materials prior to the
Department of Justice being permitted to review them,
and also to allow Case and Bryen to claim a privilege
with respect to any document(s) which they may have authored.

(b)(5)

    Upon completion of this review the Department would
be given an opportunity to review the same documents;
however, those documents for which a privilege has been
claimed, if any, would merely be identified and thereafter
we would have to issue a subpoena upon which the Senate
would vote with respect to compliance.

    I was told by Shea that a letter setting forth
these provisions and guidelines for access would be
forthcoming from the Legal Counsel.

    I told Shea I was troubled by this procedure for
several reasons.

Records ✓
Chrono
JSLisker

Buy U.S. Savings Bonds Regularly on the Payroll Savings Plan

Form OBD-197
MAY 1978

Memorandum of Joel S. Lisker, Chief, Registration Unit, Criminal Division, to Files, October
23, 1979. Cited in Chapter 6, Note 51.

(Author's Note: Information Blacked Out by the U.S. Government)

(9)

DCI disclosure
5/6/83

-2-

First, the FBI has had prior access to a number of documents from the Committee files, without following this procedure.

Second, this arrangement violates our original agreement with respect to access to witnesses who are present Committee employees and documents over which the Committee has control. We have been led to believe that the Committee would cooperate with us fully in the matter and that our access to witnesses and documents would not be restricted.

 (b)(5)

I told him that in my view the Committee was affording Bryen a special privilege which should not be given to subjects of criminal investigations, and that, in this instance, it would put us in a most difficult position since our review was designed to obtain information with which to question Bryen. This review gives him the opportunity to anticipate possible questions and concoct responses.

Finally, I asked Shea how the Counsel proposed to obtain security clearances for Bryen and Lewin with respect to Department of Defense documents. He said he was told that there is a procedure which the Committee has used on one prior occasion called execution of a "Document of Compliance". It is his understanding that Bryen and Lewin and possibly Case would be asked to sign a statement to the effect that in reviewing classified information provided by the Committee they would adhere to all requirements of the law and Committee rules for the handling of classified information.

(b)(5)
(b)(6)
(b)(7)(C)

(Author's Note: Information Blacked Out by the U.S. Government)

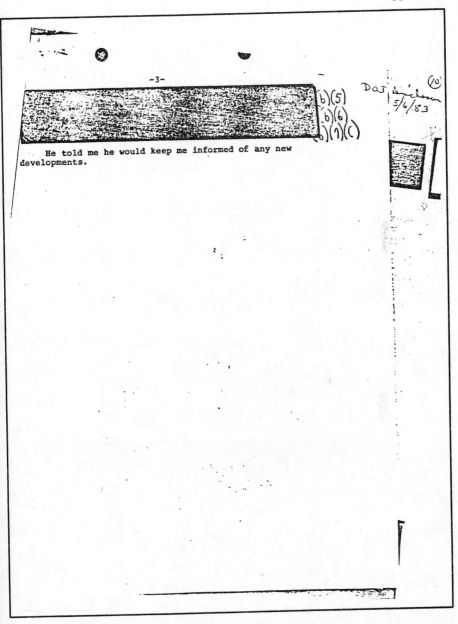

-3-

(b)(5)
(b)(6)
(b)(7)(C)

He told me he would keep me informed of any new developments.

(Author's Note: Information Blacked Out by the U.S. Government)

~~SECRET~~ ( ) 7ew DOD
DEFENSE INTELLIGENCE AGENCY   Sec 2
WASHINGTON, D.C. 20301

H

2 0 NOV 19/c

S-39,032/DB-3

TO: .Federal Bureau of Investigation
Washington Field Office
1900 1/2 Street, S.W.
Room 11330
Attn: (Mr. Timothy D. Mahoney)
Washington, D.C. 20535

SUBJECT: The Unauthorized Disclosure of the Document "DoD Analysis of
the Saudi Arabian Request to Purchase F-15 Fighter Aircraft"

1. The enclosure to this memorandum addresses two questions concerning
the unauthorized disclosure of the subject document. The answer to the
question of whether the document could be described as "a document on
bases" requires some interpretation. In a strict intelligence sense,
the document cannot be described as such. It is entirely conceivable,
however, that a person not directly involved with intelligence would
describe it as "a document on bases." Therefore, our position, is
with reservations as outlined in the enclosure, is that the document is
"a document on bases."

2. The second question addressed the intelligence value of the
document and the effect of the release of its information. Our review
of the document leads to the conclusion that it would be of high
intelligence value to the suspected recipient nation. Disclosure could
adversely affect US relations with several Middle Eastern nations, US
intelligence collection activities, future US arms sales negotiations,
the course of battle in future Middle Eastern wars, and authorized
US intelligence exchanges with foreign governments. Full details of
the intelligence value of the document and possible ramifications of
its disclosure are given in the enclosure to the memorandum.

3. The DIA analysts who were the primary contributors to this
memorandum were

~~Regraded UNCLASSIFIED when
separated from classified
enclosures.~~

~~WARNING NOTICE — SENSITIVE INTELLIGENCE
SOURCES AND METHODS INVOLVED~~

~~NOT RELEASABLE TO FOREIGN NATIONALS~~

~~SECRET~~

/

Letter of Edward M. Collins, Defense Intelligence Agency, to FBI Washington Field Office,
Attn: Timothy Mahoney, 20 November 1978, with Attachment DIA analysis of "The
Intelligence Impact of the Unauthorized Disclosure to Israel of the 'DOD Analysis of the Saudi
Arabian Requires to Purchase F-15 Fighter Aircraft.'" Cited in Chapter 6, Note 28.

(Author's Note: Information Blacked Out by the U.S. Government)

~~SECRET~~

and [REDACTED] These analysts are prepared to assist you further in any manner. you may require.

FOR THE DIRECTOR:

1 Enclosure
The Intelligence Impact
of the Unauthorized
Disclosure of the
"DoD Analysis of the
Saudi Arabian Request
to Purchase F-15 Fighter
Aircraft" (S/WNINTEL/NOFORN),
1 cy

Edward M. Collins

EDWARD M. COLLINS
Deputy Director for
Intelligence

~~WARNING NOTICE — SENSITIVE INTELLIGENCE
SOURCES AND METHODS INVOLVED~~

2

~~NOT RELEASABLE TO FOREIGN NATIONALS~~

~~SECRET~~

(Author's Note: Information Blacked Out by the U.S. Government)

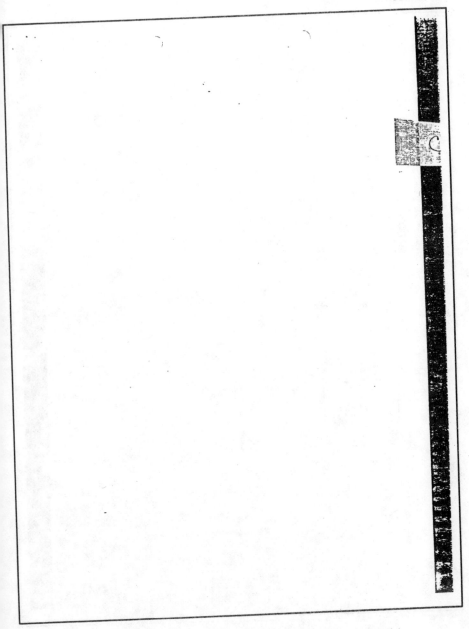

(Author's Note: Information deleted by the U.S. Government)

(Author's Note: Information deleted by the U.S. Government)

SECRET

The Intelligence Impact of the Unauthorized Disclosure to Israel of the "DoD Analysis of the Saudi Arabian Request to Purchase F-15 Fighter Aircraft". (C)

1. The document as a description of military bases.

(U) This document cannot be considered as one on military bases by any strict definition. This is because it does not contain specific descriptions, such as unit deployments, physical facilities, static defenses, access routes, precise geographical locations, etc., for any bases. The document could be considered as addressing military bases under a more liberal definition, however, since the general locations, functions, and antiaircraft defenses for all major Saudi military bases are contained in this document. It must be pointed out that the main subject of this document is Saudi Arabian military capabilities and defense requirements – not Saudi Arabian military bases.

2. The intelligence value of the document and the effect of the release of its information.

    a. Information on Egypt, Syria, Iraq, and Jordan.

(S/IMINTEL/NOFORN) The portions of this document containing US assessments of the current military capabilities and weapons inventories of Egypt, Syria, and Iraq would not be of significant value to Israel.

The information on Jordan,

is of such a general nature that it would not contribute anything of value to Israel's knowledge of Jordan's armed forces.

    b. Information on Saudi Arabia.

(S/IMINTEL/NOFORN)

This

Classified by DIA/DB
EXEMPT FROM GENERAL DECLASSIFICATION
SCHEDULE OF EXECUTIVE ORDER 11652
EXEMPTION CATEGORY.... X
DECLASSIFY ON 31 December 2008

WARNING NOTICE — SENSITIVE INTELLIGENCE
SOURCES AND METHODS INVOLVED

NOT RELEASABLE TO FOREIGN NATIONALS

Enclosure 1 to S-39,032/DB-3

SECRET

(Author's Note: Information Blacked Out by the U.S. Government)

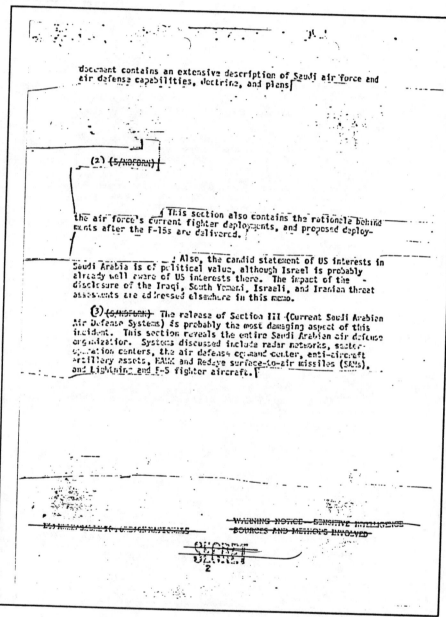

document contains an extensive description of Saudi air force and air defense capabilities, doctrine, and plans.

(2) (S/NOFORN)

the air force's current fighter deployments, and proposed deployments after the F-15s are delivered. This section also contains the rationale behind

Also, the candid statement of US interests in Saudi Arabia is of political value, although Israel is probably already well aware of US interests there. The impact of the disclosure of the Iraqi, South Yemeni, Israeli, and Iranian threat assessments are addressed elsewhere in this memo.

(3) (S/NOFORN) The release of Section III (Current Saudi Arabian Air Defense Systems) is probably the most damaging aspect of this incident. This section reveals the entire Saudi Arabian air defense organization. Systems discussed include radar networks, sector operation centers, the air defense command center, anti-aircraft artillery assets, HAWK and Redeye surface-to-air missiles (SAMs), and Lightning and F-5 fighter aircraft.

WARNING NOTICE — SENSITIVE INTELLIGENCE SOURCES AND METHODS INVOLVED

SECRET

2

(Author's Note: Information Blacked Out by the U.S. Government)

(4) (S/NOFORM) The release of Section IV (Options for the Development of Saudi Air Defense) would not be of immediate importance to Israeli intelligence. Some of the proposals given in this section are reasonably firm and would be of value, but the section is essentially a list of possible Saudi options. The section will probably gain value as time passes.

(5) (S/NOFORM) The release of Section V (Advanced Fighter Options) has probably caused little harm even though it is classified. This is because the Israelis themselves have evaluated all the US aircraft discussed in the section.

(6) (S/NOFORM) The portions of Section VI (Appropriateness of the Saudi Request for 60 F-15s) which would be of high value to Israel are the portions on absorpability and aircraft configurations.

c.   Information on Iran.

c. (S/NHINTEL/NOFORM) Information concerning the Iranian armed forces would be extremely valuable to Israel

SECRET   WARNING NOTICE   SENSITIVE INTELLIGENCE SOURCES AND METHODS INVOLVED

3

(Author's Note: Information Blacked Out by the U.S. Government)

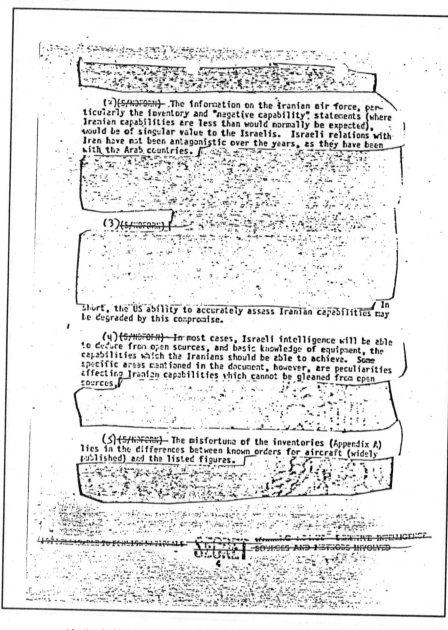

(2)(S/NOFORN) The information on the Iranian air force, particularly the inventory and "negative capability" statements (where Iranian capabilities are less than would normally be expected), would be of singular value to the Israelis. Israeli relations with Iran have not been antagonistic over the years, as they have been with the Arab countries.

(3)(S/NOFORN)

Short, the US ability to accurately assess Iranian capabilities may be degraded by this compromise.

(4)(S/NOFORN) In most cases, Israeli intelligence will be able to deduce from open sources, and basic knowledge of equipment, the capabilities which the Iranians should be able to achieve. Some specific areas mentioned in the document, however, are peculiarities affecting Iranian capabilities which cannot be gleaned from open sources.

(5)(S/NOFORN) The misfortune of the inventories (Appendix A) lies in the differences between known orders for aircraft (widely published) and the listed figures.

(Author's Note: Information Blacked Out by the U.S. Government)

SECRET ( )

d. Information on Israel.

(1) (S/NOFORN) The disclosure of the information concerning the Israeli armed forces presents an unique problem in that we are faced with the Israelis having obtained our candid assessment of their own military establishment.

(2) (S/NOFORN) Disclosure of the information on page II-16 could prove to be a major embarrassment to the US Government. Placed in the wrong hands, such information would not serve the best interests of the US Government.

(3) (S/NOFORN) Appendix A is particularly damaging to the US Government.

e. Information on other peripheral states.

(1) (S/NOFORN) The value of the information contained in the document on the peripheral states (Kuwait, Bahrain, Qatar, the United Arab Emirates, Oman, the People's Democratic Republic of Yemen, the Yemen Arab Republic, and Sudan) varies depending on several factors. These factors include the proximity of the country to Israel, the size of the country's armed forces, and the likelihood that the country would contribute military forces to any future war against Israel.

5

SECRET — WARNING NOTICE — SENSITIVE IN....
SOURCES AND METHODS INVOLVED

(Author's Note: Information Blacked Out by the U.S. Government)

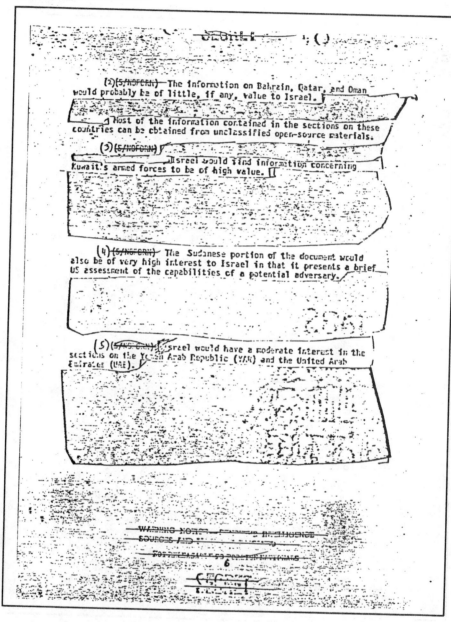

SECRET

(2)(S/NOFORN) The information on Bahrain, Qatar, and Oman would probably be of little, if any, value to Israel.

Most of the information contained in the sections on these countries can be obtained from unclassified open-source materials.

(3)(S/NOFORN)

Israel would find information concerning Kuwait's armed forces to be of high value.

(4)(S/NOFORN) The Sudanese portion of the document would also be of very high interest to Israel in that it presents a brief US assessment of the capabilities of a potential adversary.

(5)(S/NOFORN) Israel would have a moderate interest in the sections on the Yemen Arab Republic (YAR) and the United Arab Emirates (UAE).

WARNING NOTICE — SENSITIVE INTELLIGENCE SOURCES AND METHODS

NOT RELEASABLE TO FOREIGN NATIONALS

6

SECRET

(Author's Note: Information Blacked Out by the U.S. Government)

SECRET

(S/ARNINTEL/NOFORN)

This information would be of extremely high value to Israel due to the potential threat the PDRY poses to Israeli shipping through the Straits of Bab al Mandeb.

SECRET

(Author's Note: Information Blacked Out by the U.S. Government)

$\mathcal{I}$ ⑥
DOJ D~~~
5/6/53

UNITED STATES GOVERNMENT

Memorandum

TO : Files

DATE: October 23, 1979

FROM : Joel S. Lisker, Chief
Registration Unit
Criminal Division

JSL:ms
146-7-16-808

SUBJECT: Stephen David Bryen

Today at 2:08 p.m. I received a telephone call from Patrick Shea, Counsel to the Senate Foreign Relations Committee.

Mr. Shea apologized for the continued delay in making the Committee documents available for review by Registration Unit personnel. He also apologized for the delay in not sending the letter which I requested and which was to outline the procedures followed by the Committee in making classified materials available to individuals without any security clearances.

He said the additional delay arose as a result of Senator Javits wanting a letter from Senator Case authorizing the review.

I asked him if Case, Lewin or Bryen requested that we not be permitted to review any of the materials. He hesitated several seconds before responding, and then said while he would answer my question this time, in the future he would not feel bound to do so. He then went on to say that Lewin did identify certain documents for which he recommended a "speech or debate" privilege should be claimed if I requested that they be turned over to the Department.

He closed by saying that the letter I requested would come in the form of two letters. The first would authorize the review and the second would be a compilation of the agreements to abide by the espionage laws which Case, Lewin and Bryen reportedly executed. These documents would be covered by a brief letter of transmittal.

Records
Chrono
JSLisker

file forward
146-7-16-808

10/26
PGK
R LK.
1925

Memorandum of Joel S. Lisker, Chief, Registration Unit, Internal Security Section, to John H. Davitt, Chief, Internal Security Section, Criminal Division, September 26, 1979. Cited in Chapter 6, Note 19.

INDEX